Memoirs of a Vagabond

Memoirs of a
Vagabond

BONAVENTURE D'SOUZA

PARTRIDGE
A Penguin Random House Company

To order additional copies of this book, contact
Partridge India
000 800 10062 62
orders.india@partridgepublishing.com

www.partridgepublishing.com/india

Contents

Prologue   Wonder Lust vii

Chapter 1   Eil (Engineers India Ltd.) -Snam Progetti
San Donato Milanese, Italy......................... 3

Chapter 2   Premier Automobiles, Kurla...................... 13

Chapter 3   Raymond Woollen Mills, Thane 24

Chapter 4   Gajra Gears, Dewas 36

Chapter 5   Mysore Kirloskar Machine Tool
Division, Haryana 44

Chapter 6   G.k.w. (Guest Keen Williams) 55

Chapter 7   Greaves Cotton 64

Chapter 8   Djibouti - A.c.c, Mumbai 73

Chapter 9   Algeria - R.c.f., Trombay........................... 88

Chapter 10   Algeria Revisited -Star Industrial
Textile Industries, Mumbai....................... 97

Chapter 11   Italy-M/S. Stefano Stefani, Vicenza......... 106

Chapter 12   Trade Wings Institute of
Mangmt. Bombay...................................121

Chapter 13   Euro School Of Foreign Languages,
Thane... 128

Epilogue   Vision, Australia 133

PROLOGUE

WONDER LUST

Beyond the east the Sun rise, beyond the west the Sea
And east and west the wander thirst that will not let me
be..... Gerald Gould

It is a pre-independence period. The Indian subcontinent
is rocked by bloody communal riots. Arson and looting
plunder and pillage are the orders of the day. A dusk-
to-dawn curfew is clamped down upon Bombay city
(Mumbai).I look out of the window. The moon is shining
brightly in the sky. An army truck is moving slowly in the
street below. The hatch next to the driver is thrown open
and a soldier standing stiff and erect with a machine gun in
hand is peering intently around looking for the miscrants
and troublemakers. Suddenly the eerie silence of the night
is shattered by a shrill whistle from a train about to start
on its long upcountry journey from the neighbouring VT
station (CST).In my boyish imagination I find myself
hurrying along platform 11.I get into a an almost empty
compartment, grab a corner seat facing the engine. With
a final whistle the train starts slowly as it manoeuvres the

maze of criss-crossing and interconnecting tracks. Once this is over the train picks up speed, gathers momentum and rushes into the night. Station after station flashed by in rapid succession. A local train crawling on the slow track is left standing. The lights from the huts and the houses along the tracks festoon past like streamers on a Diwali night. As the train approaches the Vikhroli level crossing the hooter is sounded repeatedly as a warning. At Thane station it enters the yawning mouth of the Thane tunnel with a roar. The klickety-klick, klickety-klick sound of metal wheels rolling on metal tracks is sweet music to the ears. Emerging from the tunnel the train turns gracefully along the Thane creek. What the destination might be is of little consequence. What matters is that I am off on my long train journey.

On my way to school I have to pass the VT concourse. I see a train pulling up and coming to a stop on platform 13. I stop and wait till the driver clambers down from the engine with a leather bag in his hand containing the operating tools and as he passes me by on his way to the restroom I stare at him with open eyed wonder and admiration. Surely, I tell myself one day I will become a train driver and travel the length and breadth of India.

Sometimes of an evening we friends go for a stroll along Marine drive. I gaze at the sea with amazement. Its vast expanse cast a spell over me. It seems to beckon and lure me into its warm embrace like a seductive siren. I look at the yonder long horizon and dream of the distant shores of Genova, Southhampton and Newyork. Surely, I tell myself one day I will train as a marine engineer and working on a tramp steamer sail the seven seas.

The sea, the sea, the open sea
The blue, the fresh, the ever free.

p.s. It was not long before I came to realise my dream. On 8th September 1958,at the age of 22, I set sail from Bombay Harbour on board the luxury liner ASIA Belonging to the Italian company Lloyd Triestino to Naples via Karachi, Aden, Port Said. At Naples I took the direttissimo (nonstop train) to Rome. During the next four years I studied Philosophy and Theology at Collegio Urbano de Propaganda Fide, and at the same time I learnt to speak Italian, Spanish and Portuguese. After a brief holiday to India I flew by Swissair to Zurich where I took a train for the Quaint Old Medieval City of Fribourg. Here for the next two years till 1964, I did my diploma in French at the Institute of Modern French in the faculty of letters of the University of Fribourg and, at the same time I learnt to speak German.

PART 1

AS AN ENTERPRENUER IN INDIA

CHAPTER 1

EIL (Engineers India Ltd.) -Snam Progetti San Donato Milanese, Italy

Pressure Vessels for Madras Refineries Ltd.

On my arrival in India in 1964 I registered my name with the Italian and French Consulates General and chambers of Commerce. Nothing happened however. For the next three years, I languished in the doldrums contenting myself with mere titbits like a teaching job at Our Lady Of Good Counsel High School, Sion and ANZA (Antonio De'Souza High School), Byculla. This was followed by a 5 days Italian interpreting job for Power Cables at Vithalwadi. The big break came to me towards the end of 1967 when I was employed by EIL on a one year temporary basis as Italian interpreter for Snam Progetti. Snam Progetti had two ongoing projects: Lube India Ltd. at Trombay and Madras Refineries Ltd. Their offices were in Nirmal building, then the only skyscraper in the Nariman point area. It stood like a beckon fronting the Arabian Sea. Years later the surrounding area would be over grown and choked by an ugly and odious concrete jungle forming the commercial hub of Mumbai City.

On my first day at work I was met by Mr.Wadhwani EIL's personnel officer who took me around and introduced me to Paolo Basile, Snam Progettis's director, Domenico Montersino, his deputy Casini, Civardi and Sani. I was given a place at the end of a central pool. The pool itself was occupied by Indian Engineers, Clerical staff and 2 female typists. The left wing of the pool was occupied by the Accounts Department and the right wing by the customs dept. Under Mr.Kaulige, the only Indian officer to have charge of a department.

I was given an Italian letter to be translated into English when I heard Casini's voice calling out 'woman'. The office was in titters and the 2 female typists giggled. Waman for that was his name badly pronounced by Casini, rose to his feet, looked around embarrassed and trotted to Mr.Casini's office. A few minutes later Waman returned with his 2 arms full of blue print drawings rolled up and as he passed me he said that Casini wants to see me. When I entered his office he was pouring over some blueprints and signalled to me to sit down. Then he asked me the English equivalents of some Italian words in the blue print. Then after an hour he had finished the whole pile, he rolled up the blue prints and pushed them to one side and crossing his arms on his chest and stretching his legs he began to chat with me. He asked me where I had learnt Italian. Whether I had my fortune told by a fortune teller. Whether I had ever seen a mongoose and cobra fight. Whether I had seen the famous Indian rope trick.

At 1'o' clock was our lunch break. Most of us had our tiffins with us and some went out for lunch. Waman who was sitting next to me smiled at me and said that he was a malyaee. He said that malyalees always thought big, talked big and sometimes did it big. He said that Kerala was called God's own country. That Kerala was an only state in India and perhaps in the world to have democratically voted a communist Government to power under the chief minister E.M.S Namboodripad. He further said that what we were paid there was a mere joke not even enough to make both ends meet (though he was only a bachelor).If I was interested I should come tomorrow half an hour earlier and he would let me into 2 of his brilliant schemes called 'get rich quick'.

Next morning I arrived at 8:30.He looked around furtively, opened his drawer and removed a sheet full of numbers with a circle around number 2.This was Ratan Khatri's famous matka numbers. He said these numbers are manipulated. So if he betted a large amount on 2 as opening number he would surely get it. Then he removed the Turf book concerning the Sunday's races at Mahalakshmi. He explained to me how to pick the winner by studying the pedigree or stud of the horse, who its owner was, its trainer, the jockey who rode the horse, the handicap it carried, the distance it ran and the other horses competing with it. Thus for the next Sundays race he picked up Hard Held, a horse owned by the actor Mehmood who was known as Padosan on the race course. I gave him some money to bet on 2 and on Hard Held. Astonishingly both won and I made a small amount. But I did not pursue any further because matka was illegal and racing was addictive.

Ravi was the telex operator. He was a knowledgeable man and a good conversationalist. Whenever I was tired or had some free time I went to chat with him. One day he asked me for a small loan a week before the salary was due. I gave it to him and he repaid it promptly on the salary day. This thing continued regularly every month. I couldn't understand him why could he not stretch his money to last until the salary day. Civardi and Sani were minor functionaries and had their places in the pool. Civardi was a morose type. He always walked with his head down and when he worked his eyes were peeled on whatever he was doing. One day he let out a loud growl. I looked up and saw he had raised his hands as if in disgust. Then he said in Italian 'these Indians they are impossible'. Sani sitting next to him looked at him and grinned. The Officers looked at one another mystified.

One day I was called by Montersino. When I entered his office seated in front of him was a very nervous and high-strung Italian. His name was Cesare Miola. Montersino introduced me to him saying that he was an inspector of Pressure Vessels. Next week I would have to accompany him to Texmaco, a Birla concern, in Calcutta. There Miola would inspect the Pressure Vessel being fabricated by Texmaco. This was a requirement by Lloyd's registrar of shipping for certifying that the Pressure Vessels was explosion proof. Further, Montersino said in the course of the year a trip would have to be made to Anup Engineering in Ahmedabad and a third vessel being fabricated at Structural Engineering Works (SEW) at Mulund.

When we arrived at the airport, Miola was lugging a huge leather bag containing the blue prints of the Pressure

Vessels. When the plane was approaching Calcutta's Dumdum airport I saw clouds floating outside. Suddenly the plane lurched, shuddered and began to lose height. The plane was caught in an infernal air pocket. A ripple of panic passed through the passengers. A calm voice on the loudspeaker said 'all passengers return to your seats and fasten your seat belts. I looked at Miola. He had buried face in his hands and wonder of all wonders he was reciting the Ave Maria. Italians are not a very religious- minded people. It is said that an Italian goes to church only 3 times in his life and that too not of his own accord. The first time he is carried by his parents to the Baptismal font by the parents for baptism. The second time the spouse takes him to the altar rail for the nuptials and the third time when their body is carried by the mourners to the cemetery for burials. Soon the plane gained altitude and in a few minutes we landed at the airport.

We took a taxi to the Taj Intercontinental hotel and booked a single room with 2 beds. Then at the hospitality counter we booked a taxi for the whole day. This was my first visit to Calcutta and I was very excited about it. There was a usual hustle and bustle, the continuous honking of cars and additionally the clatter of the trams and the continuous clanging of the paddle bell by the tram driver. At the intersection the traffic policeman stood on the podium in his khaki shorts and a white shirt and a white solar topee. In his mouth was a whistle which was attached to braided cord that came through his epaulette. There was the usual crowd some walking aimlessly and leisurely, others rushing about as if they were late for an important meeting. At street corners there were usual loiterers and loafers some staring hard at the passersby, others looking vacantly into empty space.

We reached Belgharia, where Texmaco is located. At Texmaco we were met by the works manager who took us to the conference room. He was joined by his deputy and the canteen boy brought us some tea and biscuits. The tea over and the table cleared, Miola took out his blue prints which were in Italian and the works manager the corresponding ones in English. They went through it and wherever a pencil mark was made they asked the confirmation of the dimension and its allowances. This work lasted about 2 hours. Then we went to the floor shop. We crossed one shed where there was the clanging and clattering of plates and the hammering of rivets. The works manager told us that there rolling stock for the Indian Railways was being fabricated. In the next adjoining shed the Pressure Vessel stood on a wooden support. It was dripping with water and a man was standing with a hose in his hands. Miola went around carrying out a quick visual inspection of the welded seams. At times he felt them with his thumb, and then he studied the x-rays of the seams. In the meanwhile the deputy told me that the Pressure Vessel was made of thick sheet metal plates. They were then bent into a large pipe on the bending machine and the ends welded together. The 2 openings were then closed by dish ends and welded. Thus, sealing it hermetically leaving only the orifice open for the pneumatic pressure. Then the document of approval was signed.

The works manager wanted to take us out for dinner but Miola declined. We were soon in our taxi on our way to the hotel. All of a sudden I saw that there was some trouble on the road. All taxis were off the road. They were lined on both sides with the flag down covered by the black hood. As we drove on the striking taxi driver shouted at our driver, but he took a detour under the Howrah Bridge. This place was very dirty and filthy. Women were bending over the cooking pots. Ragged children were running about playing. And old men were lying on mats, some asleep and others smoking Bengali bidis. Eventually we were surrounded by the crowd and we had to abandon the taxi. The provocation for the strike was that a policeman had slapped a taxi driver.

2 rickshaw pullers came to our rescue, I got into one and Miola the other one. My rickshaw puller was a youth strong and hardy. He took off at full speed. Miola's was an old derelict man who could hardly manage a step at a time. The gap between us widened. I heard Miola shouting at the top of his voice and standing and leaning out of the rickshaw, waving to me to stop. I told my puller to stop. The moment the other one came along my man once again shot off at full speed. This continued 2 or 3 times till we reached the hotel. When Miola came down he was trembling like a leaf. Beads of sweat were on his forehead. He could hardly breathe. And then he gave me a frightful dressing down. He said that it's not enough for a good interpreter to speak good Italian but also take care of his ward. What if I had been kidnapped? I understood that he was not so much angry with me as he was frightened out of his wits. At 8 at night we came to the restaurant for dinner. There was a live band playing and a tall elegant lady with a shimmering dress reaching up to her ankles singing melodiously. A couple was dancing on the dance floor in front of the band. We sat at a table for 2. When the waiter came we ordered 2 bottles of Kalyani beer. The hotel started filling up mostly with outside guests.

When the waiter came again to take order for dinner we ordered 2 more bottles of beer. And half an hour later we had our dinner.

On our first day back in Mumbai at our office I found a deathly hush all around. I wondered why, when all at once Basile's office door opened and stepped out a fierce looking short Italian with a wisp of hair on his left eye who looked exactly like Napolean. This was Fasoli. He was in charge of the 2 projects in Italy. A man feared and dreaded by all. In the afternoon Miola was summoned by Fasoli in Basile's office and I heard his voice rise in anger. When Miola came out he passed me by, his eyes twinkled and he said with a chuckle it was the beers.

Faroukh was a tall, fair-skinned and good looking person with a squint in his eyes. The squint enhanced his looks even more. He was in charge of the dozen or so Snam drivers. His office was a space next to the telex room. Every morning the driver would gather around a table for fuel coupons and the program of duties for the day. They took the engineers to the several workshops for the inspection of goods ordered by Snam for the refinery. However their principle duties consisted of in bringing the Italians to their office at 9 a.m. from their luxurious Malabar hill residences. They took them back for lunch at 1 and brought them back at 4 to the office. In the evening they left between 8 and 9 and Faroukh could leave the office only when the last Italian left with the driver. Once a fortnight he sat with his overtime sheets filled them out and submitted them to the accounts dept. One day Montersino summoned him to his office. When he emerged he was red in the office. I later learned that he had submitted an overtime sheet for the day which was public holiday. This was only a technical error and without intent to cheat.

This was also the time when the Koyna earthquake struck Maharashtra. When I arrived at the office the lifts were shut down and I had to climb 11 floors. Even I was entering the office there was a minor shock. I felt the ground moving under my feet and the bulb that hung from the ceiling swade crazily.

Towards the end of the project I saw a short and stocky Italian around. His name was Mario. One day he was speaking to me and I saw his face was lined with grief and sorrow. He told me that during the Nazi occupation of Italy he had been rounded up with other resistance fighters by the Gestapo and dragged into cattle wagon and transported to concentration camps to Poland. Fortunately the armistice came shortly and in a few months the camp was liberated by American soldiers. The next day someone was opening my drawer and slipping a packet inside. I looked up. It was Mario. He said for breakfast he only had a cup of coffee. He was staying in Ritz hotel near Churchgate and this was his sandwiches of cheese and ham.

One day while walking by Sanjana, the pretty looking female Parsi typist called me and asked me the meaning of the word from the letter she was typing. I told it to her and when I read the letter there wasn't a single mistake. I congratulated her for this performance and she blushed pink with pleasure. While moving away I noticed that the draft from which she was typing were all in capital letters.

The project was coming to an end. The office was beginning to wear a deserted look. Chairs were empty and tables cleared and I was told to occupy the place of the dispatch clerk. One day I was registering a letter addressed to me telling me that my service was terminated.

At the end I was very happy. I thought it was a good start to a glorious innings of interpreting.

CHAPTER 2

Premier Automobiles, Kurla

Nothing could have been less auspicious than the start I made at Premiers. Just a few sheets of Fiat Standards to be translated from Italian into English. Given to me by Mr.Sringarpure the Chief Administrative officer, who then took me to meet Mr.Gopalarao an officer. He told me that they had got my name from the Italian Trade Commission as a good and reliable free lance interpreter/translator in Italian. He said that Premiers had planned to launch two new cars on the Indian roadway namely viz. Uno and Siena with the collaboration of Fiat of Turin. He said the project would continue over an extended period of time and they would need my services from time to time. He then outlined to me the immediate program. Sometime next week there would be a high level meeting between the top brass of Fiat and the Premiers management in Kurla. This will be followed by a visit of 2 technicians from IVECO a sister concern of Fiat manufacturing commercial trucks. These two technicians with Murthy a Premiers engineer and me as interpreter will be visiting HMT in Bangalore and Hyderabad for choosing suitable presses for fabricating cab parts for the 2 cars. This would be followed by a class in Italian for a select group of top officers. All the while there would be regular translation jobs to be done for the R&D dept. I could submit my bill when a single job is completed to Mr.Sringarpure who would make arrangements for its payment.

From there Sringarpure took me to the R&D dept. There I met Mr.Keravala the head of the department and seated in front of him was Mr Satpute his assistant. Kerawala said that the translations would be like the papers that I had in my hand and other technical documentation. Since the load was heavy and in order to save time, energy and expenses I could suggest the name of a Premier employee residing near my house.

We returned to Sringarpure's office which was a passage between the VIP dining room and the kitchen, of which Sringarpure was in charge. I suggested the name of Tony Domingo who passed my house everyday on his way to work. He called Tony Domingo and told him about this task and he accepted it very gladly. Sringarpure's office consisted of a table, 3 chairs and a cupboard. One of the chairs was occupied by Mr Bhandari who was the transport officer in charge of obtaining passport, visas and tickets of the officers when they went abroad especially to Italy.

The high level meeting started at 10 a.m. on the following Monday. It was attended by 2 elderly officers from the Fiat management. They were dressed in beautiful Italian suits and with silk ties to match. On the part of Premiers administration there was Mr. Venkateshan the M.D, Vakil, Kinny, Gopalarao, Kerawala and another officer whom I did not know. The Italians had deep blue coloured folders while the Indians had light coloured ones. The translations were done in the Fiat office in Turin. The work was simple as the Indians read from the folders whenever something had to be clarified they would repeat that part which I translated into Italian. The clarification given by the Italian would then be translated into English. For lunch break only the Italians and a few of the officers and me went to the dining room. It was a big room with a long table on one side covered with a table cloth. The room was painted light blue and had concealed lighting. On the opposite wall, the map of the world was painted and on it, small black balls with pins were stuck into the countries where Fiat companies operated. They were India, Brazil, Portugal and Spain. As a matter of fact the jigs, dies and fixtures for the Siena car came from SEAT of Madrid. The food was mixture of vegetarian and non-vegetarian prepared by Lawrence D'souza a veteran Premiers cook under the supervision of Sringarpure. The meeting was completed in another 2 days.

When I went to present my bill to Sringarpure he told me that next Monday in the evening, the 2 Italian from IVECO with Murthy and me would be leaving by evening flight to Bangalore. There would be a preliminary meeting in the morning in the conference room at 10 a.m. When I arrived in the morning, Murthy had a pile of HMT folders and catalogues. The 2 Italians Frederico and Romiti along with Murthy went into the conference room while I was told to wait in the anti-room. After about 20 minutes, Frederico came to the door and called me by saying psst...I was stunned by the blatant incivility of the man. He was undoubtedly handsome and a thorough racist. My response was swift and drastic. Stonewall him. Annihilate him. Behave as if he did not exist. I did not budge from my place. After a minute, Romiti came and said politely "Signore,Per,Favore,Venga". I followed him with slow deliberate steps and sat next to Murthy facing the 2 Italians. I then stared at Frederico for long time with burning anger. He asked me something to translate and I now looked at Romiti and translated it very coldly.

The next day for breakfast at Welcome group hotel, we had buffet breakfast. I love cold cuts and I filled my plate with the big sausage, rashes of Bacon and slices of ham and taking my plate sat deliberately in front of the 2 Italians. I cut off the slice of sausage, popped it in my mouth and began to chew it with relish, while I continued looking over their heads at the other guest seated around. They whispered something in their dialect but I couldn't care less.

At HMT factory the work was very simple. The three went to the showroom where the works manager showed them all the presses on display. From the choice they had made in the catalogue they identified 2 presses and after a visual check up both of the press and the technical characteristics on the name plate, they ticked it on the catalogue.

From there we were taken to the HMT watch factory. We had to wear special shoes before entering the shop floor. The place was brilliantly lighted and there were everywhere girls with white overalls and white head gear. We went rapidly around and stopped at one girl who was doing magic with her long tapering fingers which flew nimbly as she assembled the watch. To watch her (no pun intended) working was fascinating. When she took up the next watch she inclined her head sideward's and I noticed that she was a pretty girl.

In the evening we took a flight to Hyderabad and stayed at Ritz hotel. In the morning, we went to the HMT factory and the same procedure as the day before was repeated and 2 other different presses were ticked off. We were then taken to the HMT bulb factory. In the quality control room as bulbs arrived, the quality control man picked up a bulb lifted it to his eyes. He then plugged it into the wall outlet and strangely though it lighted, he dumped it in the rejection bin. We asked him about this strange fact. He replied there was a small defect which could not be tolerated because of the stiff competition they face from Philips and Osrams. Despite this they managed to make a good profit. We had a whole day to ourselves so they organised a visit to Charminar monument. It was a bitter disappointment. It was right in the middle of a road with heavy traffic around. There was continuous honking of cars and the place was filled with diesel fumes. The monument itself had almost turned grey to black with soot, grime and dirt. 2 cows were squatting sedately beside the monument and blissfully chewing the cud. All around, there was cow dung. From there we went to the Salaar Jung Museum. It was amazing how a single man could have collected so many items in his lifetime. Of the little that I can remember I found the Chinese room fantastic because of the different types of soldiers. Another piece was a marble statue of a female nude who had been just tortured and her face was all contorted in pain. Third visit was to the Golconda Fort. When we were at the top someone clapped at the foot of the fort as a warning of the approaching enemy and we could hear it distinctly at the top. In the fort itself a match was lit and the sound went reverberating until it came round to our ears again much diminished in volume.

In the evening Murthy came to my room and said he would take me next morning to an exclusive Hyderabadi hotel for breakfast. When we arrived at the hotel, I got a sharp and pungent smell of spices and the fragrant aroma of coffee. We had idlis with sambar. When we finished it my mouth was burning, and to top it all I had a piping hot and very sweet coffee. This was indeed a gastronomic delight. When we returned to Premiers, we got a bad news that there was a lock out at the factory. Workers owing allegiance to Dr. Datta Samant's trade union and those owing allegiance to INTUC had clashed. Murthy was a very worried man, because he had his house and family within the precincts of the factory.

When I went to submit my HMT bill to Sringarpure, he told me I could start my Italian classes next week. The select group consisted of seven officers. But I reminded Sringarpure of 4 bills which were pending for a long time. He turned to me and said "why do you worry Mr.D'souza. On the ground floor there is a cashier's office and the strong box contains enough cash to last you a life time". He said this cavalierly and dismissed me. When I had arrived at the Vidyavihar station for my 4th session, I hit rock bottom of depression. I went straight to the LBS Marg to the country liquor bar and I drank enough to fill uplifted. When I took my classes most of the officers had their eyes peeled to the books and I remembered one in a blur looking up and smiling at me.

When I came the next time and sat in front of Sringarpure and he said to me rather testily "what happened the other was not good. The news spread like wildfire and soon reached the ears of management. Had it not been for me you would never have been allowed to set foot again in Premiers". I looked at him for a moment and said that would serve me magnificently. I said that I have come to collect my arrears and be done with Premiers forever. On hearing this he panicked and went around looking for Kissan his personal peon. When he found him he told him to go round and bring my 4 bills with all the due signatures and stampings. Kissan returned after an hour and Sringarpure checked the bills and handed them over to me. He told me that Kissan will take me to the cashier to collect my arrears. When we went to the cashier's office Mr.Shah, the cashier was busy with some work. He looked at us for a moment and carried on with his work. We stood before him and he did not even deign to give us another look or tell us to sit down. When he had finished his work he put it aside and then took my 4 bills. He gave me another look as he scrutinized the bills. At one stage he opened his mouth to raise some objection then clamped it down shut. Having made a consolidated receipt he took my signature and gave me the money. I took the money and put it in my shirt pocket and was on the point of leaving without thanking him. However better sense and probably a better education stopped me from doing this and I thanked him and left. Accountants in Corporate houses give themselves too much air. When they pay out money they give you the impression that they are paying from their own pocket. Eventually I completed the entire course of 24 sessions of teaching Italian.

Some months later Mokashi contacted me saying that he is the new chief administrator and had a pile of documents to be translated. While on my way to Premiers I wondered what became of Sringarpure. While walking in the corridor of Premiers I met Mr.Bhandari with a pinch of snuff between his thumb and forefingers and asked him where Sringarpure was. He shook his head sadly saying that he is no more. I asked him what happened and this is the lamentable story he told me: Mr Maitreya Doshi the owner of Premiers had given a luncheon to some of his close friends. They were all Jains and therefore strict vegetarians. One of the guests found a piece of meat in his soup and Sringarpure was pulled up and severely reprimanded for this. He suffered a mild heart attack and after recovering at home in a week's time he returned to work. He found to his utter horror and consternation that he had been demoted. This triggered a major heart attack from which he never recovered.

From the very first moment I met Sringarpure I found him to be queer sort. He always wore an immaculate white trousers and a white shirt and displayed marked sycophantic traits. He was always hustle and bustle and over eager when it came to please his superiors. When it came to those below him he showed cold indifference. Such behaviour was not lost upon the attention of a very alert and well informed management. Ultimately he had to pay a great price.

I had heard of Mokashi but never met him. When I entered his office I found him to be an affable and kindly person. He pointed to a big pile of papers. I gave it one look and said that I wouldn't do it. They were all DIN Standards i.e. German Standards. I had done German translations in the past but I was never comfortable with them. He turned to me coaxingly and said that he doesn't want it tomorrow. He said to think of it this way: Do 1 page a day and there are 331 pages all marked in pencil. If you take 331 days or say 365 days i.e. one year we have no problem. When you return the translations they will be straight away filed in the R&D Dept and you will get your cheque in an hour's time. I returned in 3 months time with the work fully completed and in an hour's time I received my cheque.

One day Marius D'Lima rang me up saying he was a personnel officer of the newly constituted FIAL, which replaced PAL by majority share holding. He said there was a retired CA from FIAT of Turin. His name was Giovanni Bianchi and he needed my services as a personal interpreter for 3 months. I went very gladly and found that the entrance to FIAL in the old premises of PAL was now closer to the Vidyavihar station. Earlier it was at the Kamani end. When I approached the security office I found it to be entirely new and gleaming. The security people inside were smartly turned up and alert. Captain Gupte was in charge of security. He was a very polite and courteous man. He gave me a 3 months pass and saying to come back next day with my passport size photo affixed on it and that it would be stamped then.

When approached the office building I found there were no changes from outside. As I entered the building I thought the staircase was widened a bit or probably it was an optical illusion. When I reached the office on the first floor, there was a complete metamorphosis. The whole central pool was occupied by subcontracting firms. Among them there were a lot of Italians. Among these I found 2 girls who made it to India more because of their mental prowess than good looks. All around the central pool were the offices of heads of different departments. In the centre I found a long table with an Italian sitting at one end. I enquired about Bianchi, he pointed me to the end of the table. Hardly as I sat down, when Bianchi came, a tall elderly man full of laughter. He sat opposite me and said that from the very beginning I should consider myself as his right hand man and not an interpreter. He said we would be having 3 months of great fun and at the end probably I will have to pay FIAL rather than FIAL paying me. He had been sent to study the books for there were lot of loop holes in the past. His job was to overhaul, revamp and streamline the working of the new accounts department. He said we will start our jobs by introducing ourselves and our work to the different heads of department. Then we will summon for interrogation one departmental head after another. He told me to wipe out that smile from my face for it made me look too kind and soft hearted. When I asked a question he said you should add your beautiful English words 'where the hell were you when this discrepancy occurred? How the hell did you approve this payment without any supporting document not even a cash memo?'

Then we went to introduce ourselves from one departmental head to another. If there was a pretty female secretary, while going out from the office he would crack a joke at their expense and to my embarrassment I had to translate it. The first person whom we summoned for interrogation was a pot-bellied man wearing a faded black suit whom I had seen moving always with a mobile in his right hand. In those days mobile were rare. When he sat in his chair it seemed as though a sack of potatoes had been placed there for the whole table shook. Lunch was in the next building on the first floor in a rather small dining room and the people had to take their thalis and queue up. The food was vegetarian. There was usual rice and dal and a variety of vegetables prepared in the form of small snacks and as fruit there were custard apples very large in size bursting, very ripe and very sweet. When we were in the queue we kept an eye on those who were about to finish their lunch and went and stood behind them. One day Bianchi and I were having lunch together, a third chair was vacant when an Italian with his top crown as smooth as an egg came and sat in it. He started chatting with Bianchi, when suddenly he stopped and said"look at the man in front of you. He is eating like a wolf". I looked up and burst into laughter. It turned to Bianchi with surprise and said "HE UNDERSTOOD" and Bianchi replied serenely "he would, after all he is my interpreter".

At the end of the 3 months by the strangest coincidence both of us were scheduled to leave India on the same day. He was going to Rome by Al Italia and me by Qantas to Melbourne for a 3 months holiday with my daughter's family. We promised to meet at the airport but never could because the terminals were different.

CHAPTER 3

RAYMOND WOOLLEN
MILLS, THANE

Raymonds is a by-word and popular brand name for clothing in India, especially suiting's both pure wool and blends. Under the able leadership of Dr. G.S.Singh, Raymonds had embarked on ambitious program of modernisation of its plants at Thane. Their objective was to produce a fabric which could compete with the best manufacture in Europe. To realise this goal they went into joint collaboration with Marzotto of Italy. Marzotto had agreed to send a team of specialist for training the Raymonds personnel in the optimal use of the existing machinery and providing useful hints in the replacement of obsolete machines with new ones.

On the 1st day, I met Dr.Singh in his office and we both drove in his car to the VIP guest house. He told me that last night Silvio Trentin the leader of the Marzotto team had come to make an on the spot assessment of the conditions prevailing in Raymonds. When we entered the VIP dining room Silvio Trentin was having his breakfast. He bore a very striking resemblance to his namesake Silvio Berlusconi the chief minister of Italy. Like Berlusconi, Trentin was a tall man, gaunt and cadaverous. And like Berlusconi he was in his early seventies. Trentin was over eager to make a fine impression. We joined him over a cup of coffee and then left to make a quick round of the different departments of the factory.

We started with bale opening department under Mr.Ghosh. He had just opened a bale containing 5 micron superfine Marino wool imported from Australia. He removed a hand full of wool and held it up for our inspection. Then delving deep into the bale, he came out with the lamb's hoof and a piece of metal belonging to the hook used for handling bales and Ghosh looked at us. Trentin grinned and said it also happens with our supplies in Italy. From there we went to the scouring dept. It smelt of a rancid fat. In the centre was a long trough bubbling with hot water and detergent foams. The starting point of the trough where the hot water and the detergent were added is known as cochlea because it resembled the cochlea in our ear. The dirty wool was added to this trough and repeatedly cleaned till the wool was as white as fleece and dry. This wool can be taken away and dyed at this stage and it would be called tops dyed. From there we went to the combing dept. under Mr Gulati. He was a thick-set man and very broad bodied. When he walked towards us it was in the waddling gait. He said that the combing operation was similar to the house wife at home passing the comb through the tresses of her hair to separate different strands. The next dept. was that of spinning and weaving combined under Mr.Singh (not Dr.Singh). The spinning machines had metal points at the top for fitting the spindles. When the wool was spun into yarn it wrapped itself automatically round a spindle and when the packet was complete after a certain length and density it automatically cut off the thread and the top tilted and dropped all the packets into the aluminium bins. This yarn can be taken away and dyed at this stage and it would be called yarn-dyed. If however it continues we come to the weaving part. Here there are shuttle less looms almost all manufactured in Switzerland and the remaining from Nuovo Pignone of Italy. When the shuttles fly and struck one end they make a very pleasant sound. The weaving follows the weft and warp system. The design interwoven with the fabric is supplied by the design dept. in the form of a perforated card. As the weaving proceeds the selvedge which bears the name of the fabric and its constitution like 70-30 or 60-40 is stitched on to the fabric. Then the fabric goes for dyeing. This is called fabric dyeing. When we went to the dyeing dept. Mr Verma and his deputy Mr Joglekar were having a fierce argument. The moment they saw us Verma slipped into his office and Joglekar went to the shop floor. On Verma's table several cut pieces were ready for our inspection. Trentin studied them for the uniformity, penetration and other qualities required of the dyed fabric. We then went to the adjoining air conditioned room where sophisticated equipment was kept for preparing a more profound and accurate inspection of the dyed fabrics. Then we went to the finishing dept. The finishing dept. was under small Sehgal. He was called so, because he was really small in stature, soft-spoken, unassuming and even apologetic when he spoke. He told us that the finishing dept. is the heart of the textile factory. Here basically the 3 operations are taking place namely washing, drying and ironing (called calendaring in the factory jargon). There are different types of machines for washing the fabrics. The one I remembered now was called rope washing in which 4 or 5 outlets are there and 4-5 fabrics and each of them are fed into one hole. With one operation of the machine, 5 fabrics are simultaneously washed. From there each fabric is taken to the single drying chamber, a very long chamber and a fabric travels in it as snail's pace at a controlled temperature. When it emerges the fabric is perfectly dried. From there it is taken for calendaring (ironing).The calendar consists of a huge metal solid cylinder below it is a mirror finished basin. The fabric is fed at the fabric feed point and feed can be varied. It travels over a bed and at the cylinder, steam is injected by a system called in-out or out-in and the injection of the steam can be adjusted. The fabric then goes between the cylinder and the basin. When the machine is started the pressure is exerted by the cylinder on the fabric thus ironing it. The fabric is then taken overhead between 2 flaps and its flapping motion lets the fabric fall in perfect folds in the aluminium trolley. Standing at this point one can get a very stinging static electric shock. From here the fabric goes to the quality dept. where the room is brilliantly lit and the cloth is moved on a narrow table with a glass top below which are phosphorescent light tubes. The quality control man moves the handle and the cloth moves forward and stops. He inspects the cloth for defects and wherever a defect is found he marks it with a chalk. The defective fabric goes to the mending dept. where 40 -50 women old and young are bending over each of this fabric with the needle, thread and scissors. The mended fabric is so perfect that only an expert can differentiate from good fabric.

These mended fabrics are sold as seconds in the several Park Avenue outlets all over India. The good fabric goes to the packing dept. where it is wrapped around a flat board cut after the appropriate length label is thrust in containing the name of the fabric and its constitution. And then wrapped in cellophane and sealed by tape. These go to the wholesale dealers for inspection. Our last visit was to the design dept. This dept. is under the charge of big Sehgal. He was really fat and when he sat in his chair there was little space to manoeuvre his body. He was ably assisted by a pencil thin Parsi lady and an energetic young man called Raje. These 3 of different physical constitution worked as a perfect team. Of the many designs discussed there I could only remember the herring bone pattern. Not that I understood it but I found the words herring bone very melodious.

Afternoon we had a break for lunch in the VIP dining room. This room is divided into 2 parts by a partition. On one part is a vegetarian buffet service for Indian VIP's. The other part is non vegetarian for foreign VIP's. The service starts by the bearer bringing the tray of glasses of beer. In no other company do they serve beer in the afternoon. This is followed by other bearers bearing other types of non vegetarian dishes. In the end there was a desert consisting of rich custard pudding. This was all supervised by the cook called Pujari.

In the evening Trentin asked at what time they close. I blurted out at 6.He turned on angrily saying "ask Dr. Singh, it's not for you to reply". I was mortified but I knew it was a blunder on my part. I asked Dr.Singh and he said it was at 6. This work continued for another 2 days at the end of which there was a meeting of the top people of Raymonds and Trentin had to give a resume of what he observed, his comments and his recommendations for the future. The meeting was attended by Mr.Shroff and Mr.Kedia (both from the board of directors), Mr K.V.Iyer the MD, Khanna, Jain, Chopra and Dr.Singh. Trentin rose solemnly to his feet, gave a nod to the distinguished audience, cleared his throat and rattled off at high speed from a paper in his hand. I stared at him. He stopped and stared back at me. I asked him that this was not a speech at the United Nations. I told him to go slowly, speak out 2 or 3 sentences, pause and then let me translate. He didn't like the idea but he realised it made sense. When the meeting was over and all had left, both of us sat back chatting for a long time as though we were old chums. When I was about to leave he folded a note and thrust in my shirt pocket. Later I saw it was a fifty dollar note.

A week later Trentin was back, this time with his wife and four other specialist all retired ex-employees of Marzotto. We were 4 interpreters. Besides me there was Shirin Karanjawala, Soona Shroff and a Philipino student by name Rey. I was assigned to the Dyeing Dept. with Mr Di Marco, the dyeing master. We went to the dyeing dept. and we started our work with Mr.Verma. Di Marco was an old, stubborn and short tempered man. He had started learning english barely a month before he arrived in India. He insisted in speaking in English and it was all gibberish. I looked at Verma and Verma looked at me. I let Di Marco speak for some time until I heard a word repeated several times which sounded to me like D.A.STOOFF. I asked him what D.A.STOOFF in Italian was. He said it was 'coloranti'. I said good heavens coloranti in English is dyestuff as pronounced in English and not D.A.STOOFF as you pronounced it. I told him with a smile 'why don't you use your beautiful Italian, the Italian of Dante Alighieri and Manzoni, forget about the barbaric language of the Anglo Saxons. His face glowed with pride and pleasure. He never used an English word afterwards. At lunch the seven of us intermingled, the only exception was Rey who kept himself aloof. He had a squat body and a squat head. He stared at us without seeming to look at us. He never initiated a single dialogue. In short he looked like a Zombie. At lunch Dr.Singh pointed to the plate of fried prawns asked Rey it's meaning in Italian. He replied 'Pesci' (FISH). 'No' said the Italian next to him. He said its gamberetti. An argument ensued between Rey and the Italian. Rey kept on insisting that you can call it a fish because it comes from the sea. So when the argument was over Dr.Singh later asked me what the argument was. I told him and he replied 'probably in the Philippines, all things that are farmed from the sea are called fish. Thus oysters, crabs, turtles are all called fish.'

Mr Narayanswamy contacted me one day saying that tomorrow night at 10 pm I should catch the Amritsar Express and go to Jalgaon where they had a division for manufacturing coarse woollen blankets for the Indian army. The machine was out of order and the Italian technician and the 2 Raymonds Engineers couldn't make any headway and so my presence was necessary. During the journey Mr. Chopra will also be there. He had given me the number of the berth. When I entered the compartment he had already removed the turban and was getting ready to sleep. We arrived in time at Jalgaon. There was a company car and driver to pick us up to take us to the factory in MIDC.

When we arrived there, I found that there were 3 guest rooms. One was under lock and key for the exclusive use of Vijaypath Singhania. The other was taken by Chopra, the third whose door was open had 2 beds, one occupied by the Italian and the other was for me. After breakfast I went to the works which was just one minute walk from the dining room and I found the 3 gentlemen looking at the machine perplexed and looking at one another. As I approached the party I said 'buon giorno'. And the Italian lifted his head and came rushing at me and dragged me by the shoulder saying "tell these two gentlemen that I don't know anything about this machine. It is a machine made more than eighty years ago and I know nothing about it."I explained it to the 2 gentlemen and they said they were aware of it, he didn't even know where the start and stop button was. The roles were now reversed. The Indian Engineers began to explain about the machine to the Italian from their vast experience of the past. Once the Italian had gained his confidence, the 3 of them put their heads together and started repairing the machine.

In the afternoon Giorgio (that was the name of the Italian) and I went to the dining room for lunch. We sat opposite a man who had piled his plate with rice and added a lot of butter milk and proceeded to squeeze them into rice balls. The buttermilk was oozing between his fingers and it was a nauseating and sickening sight. We told Sheikh the cook to call us the next time for lunch after that man had finished.

In the evening the mood was upbeat, for Chopra saw the machine would now be repaired. He asked Sheikh to lay a table on the lawn with 5 chairs, and get a bottle of whisky and 5 plates of omelette and when we ended after an hour or so with our dinner the bottle was almost empty. The repair works were completed in 3 days and we were back at Raymonds. Giorgio said he had a whole day free and would love to come to my home. We took a rickshaw to Gaodevi Maidan where I was staying and on the way he asked me if there was a jeweller shop around. I took him to Vernekar Brothers on Rammaruti Road where he bought a beautiful silver ring with a sparkling semi precious stone and had it gift wrapped. At home he presented it to my daughter with all the charm and grace for which Italians are very famous. Before leaving he left his address and phone no. in Florence saying if by any chance we were to visit Italy we would be his honoured guests.

Many months later Dr.Singh contacted me saying that Raymonds had started a new project in Yeotmal with the of Calitri of Naples for the manufacture of denim. He asked me if I could come there for 3 months to teach Italian to 3 of his Engineers. I was only too glad. When I arrived at Nagpur Airport by a late night flight the promised taxi to take me to Yeotmal was not there. I rushed at every taxi that came but it was not for me. After sometime when the airport was deserted, I gave up all hope and took a cruising taxi to Raymonds office in Nagpur city. I rang the bell and the care taker opened the door. I explained to him my predicament and since the only guest room was fortunately empty I passed my night there. In the morning when the office staff came at nine, I met a lady and repeated to her my story. She was furious and immediately rang up the owner of the taxi fleet and soon a taxi came to pick me up. When I arrived at Yeotmal almost two and half hours later I went straight to meet Mr.Singh (not Dr Singh) the project Manager. When he saw me he gave a sigh of relief and he said that they were worried last night and even rang up my house in Thane and my wife said he had definitely left. Knowing that she would be in a panic I immediately contacted her by phone to say that I had arrived and she told me that she had contacted a friend of ours who volunteered to keep my wife company for the night. Mr Singh asked me to have my breakfast which was in Dr.Singh's flat. His family was with him. Then he took me to another building in the same colony and showed me my room. It was a small pokey flat with only a bed and a lot of pests that hid in nooks and crannies and hopped about like frogs setting up a racket whole night. Then in another 3rd building he showed me the room in which lunch was prepared. Then he took me to the fourth flat where I was to take my classes after 9 p.m. All this seemed to be in utter disorder because it was the starting of the project. In the afternoon I had lunch with 4 or 5 workers and it was not at all good food. In the evening the 3 engineers were joined by Dr Singh for my first lesson. After the class Dr Singh told his driver to take me to the factory site for dinner. I rang the bell and the cook was sleeping got up and looked very angry. He said all the 3 Italians had finished their dinner and gone to bed. But he was kind enough to tell me to sit down and put the plate in front of me and brought a bowl of Chicken wings which was the leftover of the evening meal. I stripped all the meat from the wings, set them on one side and the bones on the other. I ate the meat and chewed the bones and left them. In the morning when I got up I had my breakfast and realised that I had to solve my food problem by myself. So I left in search of a good restaurant. I went towards the Yeotmal station. I had to pass through horribly wretched and poor living condition. When I arrived at the station they told me that train services to Yeotmal had been discontinued many years ago and all that was a left was the masonry and a few benches on which old men sat chatting. I went back the way I had come, passed my colony and after half an hour on the highway I came to the Moghlai restaurant and to my delight saw it was also a licensed bar. I entered it and though it was only 11 o clock I ordered a biryani and a whisky. I told them not to include the drink bill in the food and return the food bill paid. In the evening Dr Singh was not there in the class but his car was there and I told the driver I wouldn't need him anymore. In the evening after class I went to my Moghlai restaurant had my dinner and some good drinks. When I walked along the highway I had to be very careful for the trucks since the road was dimly lit. Being a less frequent at highway there was hardly any traffic. There were no people walking, so I sang loudly and then looking up at the million stars in the heavens and shook my fist at then. However my teaching lasted only more than a month for the Engineers were very busy with the increasing workload.

About 2 years later Narayanswamy rang me up early morning saying that I had to attend a very urgent meeting at Mahindra Towers at 5 in the evening. He told me to drop whatever I was doing and not to fail to come. At 5 I was there at Raymonds in Mahindra Towers. In the Conference room I met a small dapper Italian with a professorial look. I spoke to him but he was very suspicious and uncommunicative. So I left him alone. When the meeting began I had to sit next to him and in the chair there was Mr.Gautam Singhania and the other members of the Board of Directors. I recognised Kedia, Mr Shroff, K.V.Iyer. The others were unknown to me. The meeting lasted about an hour. A week later, Mr K.V.Iyer rang me up personally. I was delighted for no M.D had ever rang me up at home. But when I heard what he had to say I was shocked and appalled. He asked me if I had used any rough language during the meeting. I replied coldly that as an interpreter I am just a machine and I don't remember the topic at all much less the language used. However, as a human being I live in my memories and impressions and the impression I had that day was that the meeting was a very stormy and acrimonious.

CHAPTER 4

GAJRA GEARS, DEWAS

Very little seemed to go right in this job. Pardip Ghosh of Advani-Oerlikon, Mumbai, the agent who imported the machine, Soligetto the Italian technician and myself arrived at Indore airport quarter of an hour late. The driver of Gajra Gears, the actual buyers and user of the machine, was very agitated since he had a string of duties to perform. We helped him in placing our luggage in the dicky and drove off to the Banjara hotel on the outskirts of Indore. There to my dismay I found that I had to share my room with Pardip and this went very much against the grain. Soon we were back in the car and the driver took off at a break-neck speed. The Indore Devas highway is a very busy one. Every moment a heavily loaded truck whisked past us. One truck came hurtling towards us and missed us by a hairs breath. I was seated next to the driver with my right hand gripping the back rest and I almost jumped out of my seat. It was a hot and sultry day. On both sides as far as the eye could see the landscape stretched, dry, dusty and dreary. Along the road side there were ram shackled tea shops and on benches there were people seated sipping tea. After sometime we came across a dog lying dead on the road crushed by some truck with his entrails spread over a long area. A little later I saw a speck to my left which gradually grew bigger and bigger as we approached it. It turned out to be the Tata's new factory for the manufacture of readymade leather garments specially leather jackets. It looked fresh and all around there was green grass and flowering bushes. When we arrived at the Gajra Gear reception, the lady receptionist vaguely indicated to us where the machine was lying. We had to ask our way till we arrived at the shed. We entered the shed, it was very dirty and filthy. In the centre was the average size machine covered by the tarpaulin full of dust. Solighetto ripped off the tarpaulin and a cloud of dust rose. He gave a gasp of horror. The machine was new but only in a half assembled stage. Even as he ripped off the cover nuts bolts and screws fell to the ground. It was called a circular grinding and polishing machine meant for grinding and polishing of master gears which could be later used in the mass production of gears meant for the automotive industry. I later came to learn that the machine was shipped in the unfinished condition in order to meet the delivery time schedule stipulated in the L/C. For otherwise, Gajra Gears would levy heavy penalties for late delivery. He asked for a lot of cotton waste, some spirit or petrol and the tool kit that came with the machine. He changed into his overalls and started the cleaning process. Meanwhile Pardip stood on one side his feet firmly planted on the ground with the notebook and ballpen and like a Police Constable at a murder scene started grimly noting everything that Solighetto did. After about 2 hours the Works Manager came in and stood there with his hands on his hips, surveyed the scene, then shaking his head sorrowfully walked out.

For the lunch break we had to walk about 7 minutes to the main office and climb the first floor. The dining room was very plain and nondescript. There were two ladies in splendid saris seated and having their lunch. They were there for lunch every day of our stay. I wondered if they were members of the Gajra family. The food was veg, good and plentiful. On our way back I tried to use the only toilet available, it was occupied. Somebody passing by said that there is only one toilet for the officers and everyday at 11a.m and 4 p.m. the female staff queue up to make uninterrupted use of the toilet. So I went to the workers toilet and hardly had I entered I came out rushing because my eyes were burning and nose was assailed by acrid smell of urine.

We were told to be ready at 5:30 p.m. at the office entrance and Brigadier Iyer, the personnel officer would give us a lift to the hotel since he stayed near to it. At 5:30 sharp the Brigadier appeared on the porch. He was a magnificent figure, six footer, broad shoulder with swarthy complexion and a handle-bar moustache. He stood there and surveyed the horizon over our head for some time, and then his gaze fell upon each one of us and studied us minutely. He then made majestic sweep with his hand saying "chalo..". When arrived at the hotel there was a message for Pardip from Advani's and he grimaced. We came down at 8 for our dinner. The restaurant was small and there were a few guests. There was a live band playing popular tunes. When we sat down Solighetto took out from his pocket MS Italian Cigarette packet litted and began smoking. The waiter came and we both ordered whiskies and Pardip filled his glass with the water from the jug. One of the guest asked the band to play his request. Solighetto made the request for playing of chikitita which was a very popular tune those days of which I was very fond. The next morning at 8:30 sharp we were in the Brigadier's car heading for the factory. The driver had a tendency to accelerate and the Brigadier would tap him from the back saying "dhire bhai dhire". Suddenly I heard Solighetto saying "un sommaro morto". He was craving his neck looking out for there was a donkey lying dead on the road.The Brigadier asked "what did you say?"I replied 'a dead donkey'. Brigadier said wryly tells him that this country is the country of donkeys. At the factory the work of cleaning continued. Once over Solighetto tried the power line and then the coolant line. When he opened the coolant line a horrid stench of putrefaction filled the shed. He held a basin under the coolant line and bled the line. Out popped a dead lizard. The villain of the piece. Then the first trial was started. He took a master gear fitted on to a tool holder and started grinding it. The sparks flew right up to the ceiling. There was a loud crackling noise. The gear was getting red hot so he directed the coolant jet on it. After several passes he took master gear with the tool holder and we went to the main office where the Zeiss Universal Tester was located in an air-cooled and dust free room. The readings were way off. Two more tests were carried out that evening with the same result. The next morning the grinding operations were carried out to obtain better result. When the Works Manager showed up with 2 workers and started talking to Pardip. Suddenly Pardip turned to us holding out his hands and shouting "stop stop, you have to now train these 2 workers." Solighetto who by now was very tired, ignored him. Pardip then turned to me and told me to tell him to stop. I told him so but he ignored me also. Then Pardip turned on me and said "you are not a good interpreter". Something snapped within me and I was filled with the blinding rage. I grabbed him by his shirt collar and said "you bl.bas....rd I am returning at this very instant to Bombay. I have my return ticket."All the while Solighetto was watching me. The moment I left, he also packed up and followed me. We both went to the Brigadier's office. The first thing I did was to exculpate myself i.e. I said sorry that I had used these words. In reply he said I had told Advani's that all I had needed was the Italian technician and the interpreter since he spoke his lingo the Italian would feel less homesick and bored. He told us to go and have our lunch and he would do what he could. At lunch Pardip was there but when we returned to the shed there was no sign of Pardip. In the evening we were only 2 in the car without Pardip. Pardip had been taken off the job.

Two days later a Sikh by name Kumar came in his place. He was a friendly and affable type and more interested in talking about the Sikh Community than in his work. He said that the Sikhs are unique in the world and even in the most crowded place you could spot a Sikh by his turban. How a large part of the Indian Army are made up of Sikhs. Then he spoke with emotion how in the 1960 Rome Olympics Milkha Singh had almost won the bronze medal in the 800 metre race. For dinner he objected to Solighetto's smoking. So Solighetto stubbed his cigarette in the ash tray, on the contrary Kumar joined us for whisky.

On Sunday we were in the hotel for lunch. Personally I felt like a veteran guest whereas the others were all newcomers and I was proud of it. The most of the guest were outsiders. All well heeled and rich and among them a corporator with his family. Hardly had he sat down he began striking the glass with his knife. He kept this up for some time until the waitress came running to him and he gave her a frightful dressing down. While she was almost a tremble he said loudly that all present there might hear that he had the power to shut down the establishment for inefficiency. He was hardly aware that on a dry day the management served us whisky in the jug kept at our feet.

Tired of being cooped up every night after dinner we went for walk in Indore city. There was nothing interesting as in Bombay. The only thing that impressed me was its Sodium Vapour Lighting that turned the city into a ferry land.

One day Kumar suggested that we invite Brigadier Iyer for drinks. He was only too glad to come. We requested the management to give us the empty room so that we could enjoy our drinks cosily. After sometime the Brigadier mellowed and began reminiscing of his days in the Indian Army. He said he was a member of the Indian Contingent of the United Nation Peace keeping force in Beirut, Lebanon. He spoke with nostalgia of the dances in the evening. He said that the Lebanese girls had a crush on the British army officers. The reason was obvious. They were always cleaned shaven, plentifully after shave lotioned, they bore a stiff creaseless trousers and shirt and a boots shone brilliantly.

One Sunday we went to the Mau contonment area. Everything was neat and tidy. There were beautiful buildings and neat gardens and parks. The Indian Government seemed to give the best to the Army Officers.

By Now Solighetto was very tired and fed up. The good results still eluded him. He asked me where the dancing girls are. He was looking for some entertainment. We asked one of the offices employee who said there is nothing in Indore and we will have to go to Ujjain and he volunteered to accompany us. So on a Sunday morning we took a bus starting from the hotel to Ujjain. The journey must have lasted 2 hours. When we arrived in Ujjain, the Gajra employee took us to the posh area and tapped on discretely on a door. It was open and then we entered. There in a big hall an Indian dance was in progress. The girl was petite and demeure. She had bracelets and anklets and they jingled pleasantly. All around were the musicians with their tablas and harmonium. We squatted on the floor like the rest of them. After twenty minutes Solighetto gave me a look of boredom. So when the dance was over we quietly got up, made our Namaste and left. When we were out Solighetto broke into uncontrollable laughter. He said you Indians are a funny people. Dancing girls for you people is a mild and tame affair. In Italy it would have been a wild and riotous thing. The rest of the day we strolled around a bit went to a good hotel where we had plenty of drinks and good food. In the evening we took a return bus to the hotel and all the way I was dozing off and sleeping.

At last the good results came and there was repeatability and Solighetto asked the management to send their 2 workers for training. It took him just a day to train them up and the 2 obtained repeatability. Once the management was satisfied with this, they presented a protocol in English which I had to translate into Italian and get Solighetto's signature as approval. When I told Solighetto he snatched the protocol from my hand and signed on the dotted line saying that there was no need of the translation since he had a very good bilingual secretary in Italy. Instead he had now a more important job to be done. He produced his pile of overtime sheets to be signed and stamped by the management. He presented them to Brigadier Iyer and work was done in an hour's time. Holding them triumphantly he said that he would be paid at one and half times than the normal rate.

CHAPTER 5

MYSORE KIRLOSKAR MACHINE TOOL DIVISION, HARYANA

This is the only job where the Italians were my paymasters. Oddly I have forgotten the name of the company and hence for convenience shall call them Macchine Utensili Rossi. Mr Ishwar of HEI, Bombay (Hindustan Export Import) who were the agents that imported the machine, arranged the job for me. Mysore Kirloskars were the actual buyers and users of the machine. The machine was known as Flat table grinding and polishing machine meant for grinding and polishing the surfaces of thick sheet metal plates. It was a sophisticated and state- of- the art machine because its efficiency was within 3 microns. The installation of the machine was to take place in two phases, each of 2 weeks hence almost a month. The first phase was its mechanical erection and levelling and second phase was providing its electrical and electronic connection. The names of the 2 erectors were Ottogali and Enrico. Ishwar accompanied the 3 of us to the airport to take our flight to Bangalore. On arrival at Bangalore Airport we were met by Mr.Roy, the representative of HEI's Bangalore office. Mr Roy was a pot-bellied and pompous gentleman. He came forward extending both his hands and shook rigorously the hand of one and then of the other, while he ignored me completely as though I was their valet. I was quiet upset at this but immediately I took control of myself saying that I know this type. He was one of those people suffering from an acute sense of inferiority complex hence he displayed a fawning obsequiousness towards white-skinned people while treating the fellow brown compatriots with utter contempt. At the Welcome group hotel he shepherded them straight to the bar where he offered them a welcome drink. Once again I was totally ignored. The moment he left and I was in my room I dialled room service and ordered double whisky on the rocks. At dinner also I had a drink with Italians. Back in my room after dinner I ordered another drink and went to sleep. In the morning I had a stupendous hang over but absolutely no remorse nor regrets. When Enrico went through the bills he saw my 2 liquor bills and looked at me and I said they were mine. He only smiled back. In the private taxi I sat next to the driver and looking back at the 3 sitting behind, I told them not to disturb me and I went to sleep. I got up at Davangiree where the 4 of us went to a restaurant to have our lunch. I recommended Biryani to the Italians since it was non-veg and not so spicy. After the meals Roy picked the bill to pay. In another ten minutes we reached Harihar. Mysore Kirloskars had vast grounds and was fully surrounded by a wall. Over the entrance the name of the company was in bold relief, each alphabet made of wood. Inside we first came across the guest house, behind that there was an officer quarters and still behind there was a sprawling factory. At the end of it was beautiful trimmed golf course. I thought to myself that Mysore Kirloskar officers were a pampered lot.

The guest house was run by a contractor named Hussain. He led us to our individual rooms. I had a big room with two beds, each with a mosquito net curled up and a fan in the centre. The thought of the mosquito net bothered me, no matter how good the net was a mosquito always managed to slip in and wreck your sleep. I was arranging my things when Enrico came to me with a bottle of red sweet Marsala wine and gave it to me. We exchanged a few words and then he patted me on the shoulder and left. It was his gesture to say that he understood me.

Roy then led us to the factory where we were met by Dixit, the Engineer assigned to us during the two weeks. The table grinding and polishing machine was at the very entrance of the factory. Its grouting had already been completed but when the air bubble gauge was applied at every point of the table it was completely out. They had hurried consultation and it was decided that the grouting be completely dug out and removed and fresh cement poured in. This was the work that would last several days. In the meanwhile I went on my curiosity round. All kind of machine tools were there. They all operated at the same time setting up a deafening cacophonous din. The machine tools consisted of lathes, milling machines, drilling machines, boring machines, machines for drawing wires and machines for making plates. Besides there were machines for making elbows, bolts, nuts and screws. Dixit joined me and explained to me that a machine tool industry is fundamental to all other industries. It is first and basic industry which supplies all the possible parts to manufacture secondary machines.

For evening dinner we had a choice of eating out in the veranda or in the dining room. We wisely thought of eating in the dining room because Harihar is the Mosquito infested place. For dinner there was a dish of chicken. It was badly cooked and the cook had chopped it into small bits and put everything including the feet and claws. I brought this to the attention of Hussain and he promised not to repeat it. Next morning for breakfast I saw that Ottogalli had haggard look. He said he hardly slept because whole night a dog was barking somewhere on the grounds. Its barking grew into a howl. And finally his howls became very frantic. Ottogali thought that an earthquake was about to strike the area and that kept him awake. In the morning however he fell into restless sleep.

Roy came to me and said he was returning to Bangalore and would send Sunder, an Engineer in his place. He asked me to inform the Italians. I replied that you can do it yourself. You have managed so far by yourself but he turned a pleading look towards me and said please do it for me. And at last I relented. The next day Sunder turned up around midday. He was a young man full of verve and vigour and came bouncing into the factory. He shook hands warmly with every one of the eight or nine men standing around the machine then going to one corner stood watching the work in progress. In the afternoon when I went for lunch, I went to my room to wash my hands and there I saw a bag on the other bed. It was Sunder's. I waited for him and told him that the room was exclusively for my use and it was paid by the Italians. And that he should go and meet Hussain and take another room. He remonstrated with me saying that

Roy had told him to do so. I told him angrily "Roy be blown and please do what I tell you" and he went away.

One day an officer working in general administration by the name of Hebbar came to the factory and met me saying that he had heard the interpreters name was D'Souza. He came to find out if I was a Mangalorian or a Goan. I replied that I was a blue blooded Mangalorian born in Mangalore but brought up in Bombay. I asked him if he was related in any way to the famous painter Hebbar. He beamed as he said yes but a distant relative and I implicitly believed him for he was a man without guile. Before leaving he invited us for breakfast at his quarters. He came to pick us up at 8 next morning and went to his quarters. There we met his wife, a quiet retiring woman whom I heard speaking Tullu with her husband. It's not that I can understand Tullu but I can recognise it when spoken. The breakfast she had prepared was fantastic. Fluffy Idlis, chutney made from coconuts of coastal region and sambar just spicy enough. Not even the most renowned Udipi hotel in Bombay or Thane could boast of such a wonderful breakfast.

One day the 2 Italians opened the wooden crate containing the machine and shipped by container from Italy. They took two packets of Pasta Barilla. They met the cook giving him instructions how to prepare the Spaghetti. When we sat for afternoon lunch the Spaghetti was served and it was a very spongy and sticky mass. Towards the end when the erection of the machine and its levelling was being completed Dixit invited us for evening tea to his home in the city. His wife had prepared some usual Maharashtrian sweets. They were delicious and we had tea after that. Dixit then thanked the 2 Italians for the sincere and hard work and turning to me paid me the finest compliment I had ever received. He said that during all the discussions in the factory not once was he aware of my presence. The to and fro conversation moved like a crystal flow. And I added rather vain gloriously "yes, some interpreters are interrupters".

Towards the end Mr.Roy showed up and gave me a quartered kilo Darjeeling tea saying that it was the best in the World. I thanked him for, knowing that he was making up for his boorish behaviour in the past.

A week later I was going to the airport to take a flight to Bangalore with Walter Berutto and Olivetti both of them Electrical and Electronic Engineers. Accompanying us in the car was Ishwar. Berutto dropped a bomb shell when he spoke to Ishwar in perfect English and without any accent. He said he had a big row with his boss about the desirability of having an interpreter this time. His boss insisted that the report from the previous 2 about the interpreter was good, paying an interpreter in India cost them only peanuts. Besides you never know what emergency may arise and you may then need one. Hence he was compelled to have one. I felt humiliated hearing this but a line from the poet John Milton on his blindness "they also serve who stand and wait". Thus watchman, fireman, serviceman during peace time all of them do nothing but wait and watch and are paid their salaries. All I had to do was follow the leader keeping one step behind him.

At Bangalore airport we were met by Sunder. There was no any fuss this time. The only thing I observed was that Walter Berutto and Sunder got on very well and became fast friends. Their friendship was broken only on the last day of our departure for Bombay with the announcement (last call for boarding the flight to Bombay). The next morning we took the private taxi to Harihar. This time I was awake and I remember passing through Tumkur and Chattisgarh. We went straight for our lunch to Mysore Kirloskar without stopping at Dawangiree. In the guest house I occupied the same room. Every day for breakfast, lunch and dinner only English was heard. Olivetti and I were mere spectators.

One day there was a major break down in the machinery and Berutto had to seek help from his boss in Italy. We were directed to go the conference room where we would be connected to Italy when the call materialise. While Olivetti and I sat down comfortably, Berutto and Sunder waited anxiously for more than two hours when Berutto got his boss on the line. Once the call was over Berutto and Sunder looking at each other slapped their right hands across and their left hands across as though the crucial goal had been scored at an International Football game. After a week or so the management arranged a picnic for us and the place was either Jog Falls or Humpy. Finally Jog Falls was decided. Hussain had given us a hamper and we left early morning for Jog Fall. As we went on we came to a place where both sides there were a cultivation of giant sized Sunflowers. It was an unforgettable sight and I have always wondered if this land belonged to manufacturers of Saffola cooking oil. At Jog Falls there were other Indian tourists and I noticed whenever Berutto passed girls turned to look back at him since he was tall and good-looking.

After a wonderful picnic at Jog Falls Berutto, Olivetti, Sunder and I returned to Mysore Kirloskar. Jog Falls reminded me of an Italian interpreting job done in Karnataka Veneers and Plywood Company some fifteen years ago at

Telaguppa. This was a worst interpreting job in my life. Italian and I were staying at the two Government Dak Bungalows at Jog Falls. I arrived at Telaguppa by flight up to Belgaum. There the Karnataka Veneer company car took me to the factory at Telaguppa. There I met Dyaneshwar, a surly, old, cantankerous gentleman. I requested him if I could telephone my wife that I had reached safely, but he said that he would tell his principles in Bombay to inform my wife which he never did. The Italian had a small furniture making factory in Rome. He showed me the catalogue and the furniture was exclusive all made of teak wood. He had come to Telaguppa to import teak wood.

It was the monsoon time and it rained in torrents and without ceasing. Every morning the two of us left in open Jeep for half an hour. One morning something pricked my leg. When I touched it I found it to be a slimy creature and a shudder ran down my spine. I tried to put it out it did not come then I gave it 2-3 hits before it was flung on the road. The driver told me that it was a leech. At the factory we had our breakfast in the kitchen apart of which was temporarily converted into a dining room. After we went to the adjoining factory where the teak wood veneers were sliced. This was because the Indian Government had banned the export of teak wood in logs but taking the teak wood in the form of veneers was permitted. The slicing of the veneers was the laborious process. Heavy salt incrustations were embedded in the wood in the trunk and these had to be removed. They used all kind of implements to remove them. Once the log of teak wood had been put in the machine had to be completed the very same day otherwise leaving the log for the next day would be damaged. This work sometimes continued till late in the night. Both the Italian and I had nothing to do. We couldn't go out of the factory because of the rains. All we did was to move around the other machines and come to see our machine to see the progress made. It was frustrating as there was hardly any progress. Once both the Italian and I went to the other end of the factory where some extension work was being done. There the Italian amused himself by ogling the female construction workers. Our lunch was at one and dinner at 8:30 but we couldn't start our meals without Dyaneshwar being present with us. One evening we waited for him till 9 o clock still there was no sign of him. I told the cook to give us our Quota of whisky and the dinner. Hardly had we begun Dyaneshwar appeared in the dining room and he gave me a long dirty look. Then he joined us and we all ate in silence. When we were about to leave after the completion of the work he called me and said that the Italian was going to Bangalore by car from there he would take a flight to Delhi and then on to Rome. He said there were three other officers going to Bangalore for important work and there was no place for me. He suggested that I go down to Sirsi and take a Karnataka State road transport bus or a private Canara Pinto or a Ghatge Patil bus to Bombay. I listened to him and nodded. On the day we were to leave I stood next to the car with my bag and once the four people had entered I told the officer in the front seat to push up and I sat next to him with the bag on my lap. Once again Dyaneshwar gave a long dirty look. Once we started on our way after half an hour the driver stopped the car and taking the bag from my lap and put it in the dicky. There was only one driver and he was over worked. Every now and then his head nodded because of lack of sleep. At one stage we nearly collided with the truck coming from the other direction had he not swerved the car at the last moment. At Bangalore I stayed in the cheap hotel and next morning I went to the Indian Airlines and changed my Belgaum –Bombay return ticket to Bangalore-Bombay ticket paying the difference.

Once after a very difficult day at the factory, Berutto and Sunder were in no mood to talk in English. To speak foreign language for an Italian all the time it's very taxing affair. We ate in silence. After our dinner Berutto gave me along searching look and lowered his guard. He broke into Italian saying how he envied me as a freelancer. He said that his boss was a tyrant. Not a single day passed without some serious quarrel. He had often thought of migrating to France for his wife was French. But that would not solve his problem because the French loathed the Italians. Everyday hundred of Italian workers travelled by local trains to the border station of Ventimiglia where the Italians crossed into France to work in the numerous French factories there. Besides there is a question of getting a job and then it would be in a subordinate position. Hence it would like the fish in the frying pan finding the heat too much jumps off the frying pan and lands straight in the fire.

Towards the end the wooden crate was ripped open completely. In it there was a coffee percolator for two, an all-purpose device with a bone handle consisting of a coxcrew, a tin-cutter, pen knife, etc. and a dozen cute small plastic boxes each containing a different spice, all this Berutto gave them to me.

When the job was coming to an end he asked me for my bill. On submitting the same he changed the rupee into dollars at the actual rate then and said he would pay me in dollars. An alarm bell rang in my mind. I was reminded of Anil Trivedi who had once accepted dollars from some Spanish party and to his horror found that they were all fake. My suspicion was roused when Sunder insisted that I take them in dollars and change them in black market at M.G.Road and I would get an amount. I said taking foreign currency was a crime and I knew no dealer in foreign exchange. So I contacted Dixit who lent me his car and the three of us went to the local branch at Bank of India. I waited at the reception while Berutto and Olivetti went inside with the passport and emerged half an hour later with Indian Rupees.

We were to leave at 10 a.m. next morning after breakfast. We were having our breakfast when the message came from the factory that the machine had gone hay wire and not functioning at all. Immediately the two Italians and Sunder left their breakfast and went to the factory. I did not budge from my seat. When they returned Berutto asked me if I could stay a few more days."No way at all. I have been fully paid and don't intend to continue. Besides you speak English very well so where is the problem". So they went into consultation with the Kirloskar people. At last they returned saying they were leaving with me. I have no news as to the outcome of the machine. But of one thing I am very certain. Berutto and Olivetti must have returned to India after two weeks and set the machine in working condition and this time, without the presence of an interpreter. It all goes to show that the services of an interpreter are not absolutely indispensable.

CHAPTER 6

G.K.W. (Guest Keen Williams) –

A Press for the fabrication of Cab Parts
for Ashok Leyland Trucks

I arrived at the G.K.W. Head Office in Bhandup ten minutes late. When I entered Mr Bapat, the Managing Directors office, I found 4 people seated there gloomily in an atmosphere of suspicion and mistrust. They were Mr Bapat, Fernandes the Personnel Officer and the 2 Italians by name Andreotti and Danilo. After the exchange of customary greetings Danilo pointed a quivering finger at Fernandes saying that all the way from the airport to Bhandup this man had not seized to call us Mafias. Fernandes understood and laughed. He said I was only trying to make conversation with them by asking them if they had any Mafia friends in Italy. I translated and Danilo became even more angry saying that they came from Milan in Northern Italy whereas the Mafias were all bumbs and brigands to be found only in Southern Italy to which the northerners derisively referred to as a part of North Africa. Once the cloud of misunderstanding had lifted and the atmosphere was clear Mr Bapat said that we could leave for Cane. It was long way off and the private taxi and driver were waiting for us. At Cane Mr Ramaswamy the works Director or Mr Waghale would be waiting for us. We left straight away and as we approached Cane after Lonavala the driver told us that he would be turning left towards the train's level crossing. If we continue on the straight road we would come to Taloja where the Venkys Chicken farm and Eagle Flasks Factories are located. At the level crossing we waited for quite some time until the train from Pune thundered past to Bombay. The level crossing gate opened and we along with some vehicles, Cyclist and Bullock carts went across. In the distant plains I could see a small one floor structure which was the guest house, then at quite some distance from there were a cluster of houses belonging to the officer and still further the medium sized factory.

At the guest house we were met by Mr Waghale and elderly man with a very red mouth due to much chewing of paan. He took us to the first floor and showed us our 3 rooms. On our way back he said that on the ground floor there were two rooms occupied by East German technicians from Erfurt (GDR). Besides every morning we would be having our breakfast there in the dining room. From there we went walking for about 10 minutes to reach the factory. When we entered inside we found in the centre the huge giant press and at the other end were 3 German technicians working with the grave air on 4 very small presses. Ramaswamy joined us. He said that the Italian press was a very best available in the world. It was in demand in all leading Automotive Industries. When once it was delivered it remained idle for more than a year for there were not enough Italian Service Personnel to commission them. Mr

Ramaswamy said that this press is known as a 5 ton double action press. The 2 Italians said about inspecting the press. Andreotti removed the plate from under the press covering the floor and descended below ground level while Danilo went to the platform next to the Control panel. After nearly an hour they had finished their inspection we had a joint consultation. Andreotti that the pneumatic pressure line was entirely choked by rust and extraneous matter. Danilo said 2 electric switches were out of order. All this work would take quite some time and the 2 Italians asked for a Walkie-Talkie in order to facilitate communication from underground level to the panel. Mr Ramaswamy suggested that we could have meeting every three days to review the progress made.

In the afternoon we had our lunch in the common dining room where both workers and officers sat together. The food was only rice, dal and cabbage and it was self service. The 2 Italians came to our table with their food. Each one looked at their plate then at each other and passed some commands in their dialect. Waghale understood the meaning and hastened to reassure them that in the evening we would be having good food in some restaurant outside. In the evening we left at eight in the company car. At the level crossing we had to stop a long time. First one train passed from Bombay to Pune and after sometime another train passed from Pune to Bombay. At last the gates opened and heavy traffic moved out in both directions. We drove quite some distance on the Bombay-Pune road before we stopped at some wayside restaurant. Trucks were parked outside and when we entered we saw the drivers eating in one corner and chatting noisily. The restaurant was a third class restaurant. We asked for the menu card and there was none. I had to explain to the Italians whatever was available and they settled for plane rice and some salad which was sliced onions. Andreotti had brought a bag with him and from that he removed a small tin of "Olio di Sasso" (olive oil), Vinegar, Pepper and Salt. They sprinkled the rice generously with olive oil and vinegar and shook on it pepper and salt mixing all this thoroughly they began to eat. When we were back in the guest house we sat on the sofa in the living room outside our rooms and there Danilo, the senior of the 2 began to crack jokes laden with sex with much lurid details. Thus we passed a pleasant one hour before retiring to bed.

The next morning we came to the ground floor for breakfast. The East Germans had already left and the breakfast table had not been cleared of the bread crumbs. We waited until the canteen boy arrived and cleaned the table. He then went back and came back after a quarter of an hour with pot of boiling tea, slices of bread and a tray of butter. The 2 Italians looked at the breakfast and said to me "you have an English tradition. Where are the bacon and eggs?"Waghale assured them that tomorrow they would get fried eggs. The next morning there were no fried eggs for breakfast. Danilo looked at me again and then at Waghale and turned to me and said "you got your independence in 1947.Still you remain an underdeveloped country. This touched me in the raw. I exploded and told them that Italy is a worst country in Europe. Every 4 to 5 months a your government falls. Your public transport system is a disgrace in Europe. Every now and then they go on a eleventh hour lightning strike bringing the trains to a grinding halt and the commuters are stranded at different points.

Your national carrier ALITALIA is an acronym in English meaning "always late in takeoff, always late in arrival". Both of them understood nothing of the acronym. So I had to explain it to them. It was difficult and troublesome. Finally when they did understand the meaning of the acronym they burst out laughing and I too laughed at them. Thus peace was established.

In the factory I had nothing to do so I went out. In the far away distance I could see the highway and some traffic moving on it otherwise there was no life around. I went around the factory and on the first floor outside the window of Ramaswamys office there was a beehive but no bees in it. Back in the factory I saw the two East Germans and decided to go there. Here there was no Berlin War to be breached. No Check point Charlie to pass through. And so I crossed over leisurely. When I stopped I looked at the East German and gave them a smile and they both gave me a curt nod of acknowledgement. Two days later when the East Germans had left for lunch at the guest house (they ate all their meals in the guest house by themselves), I excused myself to Danilo and Waghale that I was going to the toilet. When I arrived at the guest house, I opened the door and said "guten Morgen, meine herren (good morning gentlemen) ".They both looked up startled and seeing me one of them pulled out a chair and laid a plate for me and pushed a tin of tuna fish and a tin of cocktail sausages with bread and butter and asked me to have a sandwich. The other went to his room and fetched a bottle of Vodka saying that it is a genuine Russian stuff. I declined the vodka and they said they 2 have it only at night. Sandwich was good but I found the tins and the Vodka bottle made of shoddy material. As a matter of fact the Vodka bottle seemed to be made of smoked glass and a label was affixed awry.

As the work was slow Danilo told Ramaswamy that they would be working also during the night and requested the Indian Engineer to be present. Mercifully my presence was not required. When the press was finally cleaned and was running on idle perfectly well the Italians phoned their principles in Italy and said they were returning for a 2 weeks rest and holiday.

2 weeks later I was back in Bapats office. There I got the bad news that Mr Waghale had suffered a major heart attack in his Chembur home and passed away. They were not able to find a suitable replacement in the meanwhile. The 3 of us left as before and as we were reaching Khopoli I remembered the stud Bar and Restaurant. It is the favourite watering place for rich Bombayites when they drive to Pune for their weekends. I asked Danilo if we could stop there for some snacks. He stoutly shook his head and said no, that we are already 2 weeks behind schedule and couldn't think of losing more time. As we came near Stud Restaurant I repeated my request but again a firm no. When we reached I told the driver to stop the car and open the dickie and took my bag out. Suddenly both the Italians seeing this got alarmed. They came out and I told them "you can go ahead with your work I am returning home." Instantly they relented and said I could have my snacks while they waited out. I told them to come in and sit down and the waiter brought each of us a menu card. I ordered a beer and some cheese sandwiches but however the Italians declined the beer but had cheese sandwiches instead. When the bill came I paid it and left a tip. Italians are very hospitable in their

country but when they go abroad they are very tight twisted. It was not their love for work as much as their fear of paying that made them refuse my request in the first place.

When we reached Lonavala the driver said he was turning left to Fariyas Hotel. I asked him what for. He said the Italians were putting up at Fariyas during their stay. It was for an unexpected thunderbolt. I least expected Bapat to practice the South African style segregation and apartheid policy on me. Had he told me this in Bhandup I would have fought with him and even threatened to go away. But here it was too late.

The Italians were down in 5 minutes and when we reached Cane I told them to first drop the Italians at the factory and then me at guest house. At the guest house I found out that the East Germans had finished their work and left. Now I was saddled with the unhappy situation of being alone in the guest house where once we were 5. I later learned that the East German Counsellor Car had driven up to the guest house. The luggage of the 2 technicians was put in the dickie and the 2 East Germans were bundled in the rear seat of the car and the car drew off straight to the airport. Thus giving them no possibility of effecting a defection. Honecker, the communist boss of East Germany's tentacles reached even a remote village in Cane in Maharashtra to control his citizens.

In the afternoon I had to have my lunch all alone. The Italians said they would have only one sumptuous meal in the evening at Fariyas. In the evening too I ate alone. This time however there were fewer people in the dining room. I walked along the dimly lit path to the guest house and when I opened the door I was surrounded by pitch black darkness and the silence of the grave. All of a sudden the fact that I was all alone struck me frightfully and forcibly I rushed to my room on the first floor and I entered and switched on the light I saw or at least I thought I saw that goblins were dancing on the wall. I looked up at the Ceiling and there I found an army of goblins, gremlins, banshees and pixies massed together and about to launch an attack on me. A very fat and load some banshees was thumbing its nose at me and mocking me. I switched off the light, changed my clothes leaving my pant and shirt as a litter on the ground and wearing my sleeping pyjama and shirt I jumped into bed pulling the coverlet over my head. I stayed still, waiting any moment to hear footsteps approaching towards me. I was really frightened out of my wits. Suddenly I remembered a passage from a book of Psychology that under such conditions as now I should say some prayer and concentrate on my breathing. I said a 'Hail Mary' and concentrated on: breathe in breathe out, breathe in breathe out and soon I fell into deep sleep. Towards morning I heard a whistle blowing somewhere in that large estate and another whistle replied from the opposite area of the first in reply. These were the Security people patrolling the area. Reassured also on the real fear of Burglars and thieves I now fell asleep.

The perfidy of Bapat towards me rankled at the back of my mind. I wanted to get even with him. So one evening while the Italians were going back to the Fariyas hotel I asked the driver that I too was coming if he could wait for me till the dinner was over. He said he could not wait without Ramaswamy's orders. So the next day I told Ramaswamy that one of the Italian had asked me to come for dinner since he had some problem with his food and the waiter. He readily agreed. The next night I was having my dinner at Fariyas with the 2 Italians. For dinner I ordered my favourite items: Mulligatawny Soup with garlic bread, fried chicken with finger chips, salad and finished with 2 scoops of Vanilla Ice-cream with hot chocolate. Thus I ate like a Lord and revenge was sweet.

When I came out of the hotel the driver & the car were not there.I waited for sometime & was about to turn in at the hotel when I saw the car coming in. I sat next to the driver he was very silent & morose. I spoke to him in Marathi asking him his family details & he felt happy. At the guest house I gave him a tip & he was very pleased. On the day we left I had half a mind to get down at Thane and go home, but thought better of it. I accompanied the 2 Italians right up to Bhandup. Not a word did I speak to Bapat about his perfidy instead I went round looking for free type writer and finding one I typed out my bill and submitted it to Bapat. Thus I saved the bother of going to the Post Office and also gained some days where payment is concerned.

CHAPTER 7

GREAVES COTTON

Offshore drilling bits for ONGC

I had often read about the struggle between the Burgoisie and the Proletariat. It was for the first time that I witnessed in Greaves Cotton that tug-of-war between the management and the workers.

Mr Deodhar the Works Manager of Greaves Cotton, Roberto an expert welder from a leading association in Italy and myself,we had just finished our lunch at a posh hotel near the airport. We then took a private taxi to Nashik. Its a journey of nearly 4 hours. While travelling Mr Deodhar told me what was expected of us at the factory. He said that they supplied the offshore drilling bits on the regular basis to ONGC. The drilling bits were huge made up of welded parts and of late hair thin fissures were detected in the welded seams and were hence rejected by them. For quite some time Greaves Cotton tried to get a good welder from Italy but without success. They had contacted the Italian Consulate, Italian Chamber of Commerce and the Italian Trade Commission. Finally it was the Italian Chamber

Of Commerce who gave this contact with the welders association and Roberto's name. Robertos service, being an expert welder came very costly. Then there was a long Pause. I thought that Deodhar was brooding about something. Finally he said that Greaves Cotton had gone through a very difficult period in the past. There were regular confrontations between them management and the workers. Now with most of the workers demand being met the situation was stabilised and there was peace. I later learned that Deodhar himself during one of these altercations had been dealt a severe blow on the back of his head with a metal piece given by one of the workers thus fracturing his skull. He was given first aid treatment in one of Nashik's hospital then later recovered in a prestigious hospital in Bombay. All this trouble was created by the leader of the workers who was a learned person and came from one of those Southern States where Marxist ideas and communist dialectics are rampant and widespread.

We were put up at VIP hotel on the periphery of Nashik. Next morning at 8:30 sharp Deodhar came in his private car to pick us up. We drove to MIDC where Greaves Cotton was situated. When we approached the factory I grew very apprehensive. But there were stringent checks by the security and then only we were allowed to enter.

The drilling bit was really a monster probably weighing several tonnes. In no way was it comparable to the small drilling bits brought by Electricians and Masons when they come to our homes for repair. Immediately the welding machine and electrodes which were used for the drilling were checked by Roberto and the work of repairing started. As Roberto was examining the X-rays of the welded seams

I saw a tall, be-spectacled man with a kerchief round his neck and under his collar worn like a Bandana. Puffing a Bidi in his mouth coming towards us with a swagger. He was completely oblivious of his surroundings and walked past with an air of complete disdain. This was the leader of the workers.

After 2 days the Deputy of the leader of the workers told us that there were would be meeting in the evening addressed by their Trade Union Leader. Hence there would be no work and Roberto as a foreign worker had to attend it. I was free to attend or not to attend. The meeting was addressed by a Christian Labour Leader from Mulund who spoke pure and chased Hindi. He first said a few words welcoming our Foreign Brother Worker from Italy and went on with the agenda of the meeting. At the end of the meeting the Union Leader, the Leader of the Workers, his Deputy and the 2 of us went in a taxi to the VIP hotel for tea and snacks. There they discussed about the picnic to be held on next Friday. Friday was a day when the factory was closed because of power shortage.

On the day of the picnic, the leader of the workers and his deputy came to the VIP hotel and fetched us. It was a long drive to the picnic spot. The picnic spot was a eucalyptus glade, dripping with freshness and the fragrant smell of eucalyptus. Nearby a brook gurgled and murmured as it floored over stones and pebbles. It was almost a piece of paradise on earth. Most of the workers were already arrived, they had spread papers, tarpaulins and even bed sheets. The food was brought by the caterers and we all started making merry. The bottle of whisky was brought out and passed from person to person. 2 tumblers were given to us by some of the workers and we all began to eat and drink and have fun. By evening except for 2 workers, who were teetotallers, the rest of us had all reached different degrees of intoxication. One worker was fully drunk and I was tipsy and happy. The next day when we arrived at the factory, the worker who was fully drunk the previous day was still fully drunk and was refused admittance to the factory. He was standing at the gate and talking to a friend of his inside the factory.

The next night Roberto and I accompanied Deodhar, his deputy and their wives to a Dabha for dinner. Deodhar told me that it was the best Dhaba on the Mumbai Pune road and one had to make reservations a few days in advance. When we arrived there, there were already some private cars outside the Dhaba. We entered to find the place very clean and tidy. The food was excellent and the conversation was all a mixture of English, Marathi and Italian. There were drinks but wisely I declined it. This was the managements answer to the workers picnic.

Next day Deodhar called me and told me to request Roberto to stay a few days longer. Instead I went and asked Roberto to accompany me to Deodhars office. I told Deodhar that he should tell it directly to him and I would translate which is the right procedure. Roberto refused absolutely saying that when you left Italy for India, his mother was very upset. Deodhar refused his excuse. The Italian gave another excuse saying that he had another welding job to be done in Italy. This excuse also was turned down by Deodhar. The Italian then said that he was bored and homesick. Deodhar shook his head. Finally Deodhar offered him extra pocket money which need not be mentioned to his boss. Roberto reflected for a moment, smiled and finally accepted to stay.

During those 3 days, Roberto trained one more worker besides the earlier 2 in which he called the proper art of welding.

When we were to leave, Deodhar gave us the good news that Indian Airlines had started the Avro flight from Nashik to Mumbai. With this we would be doing without the 4 hours car journey which is not only a tiresome for the body and also for the mind. We arrived at the airport which was an open field with a shed as a Hangar on one end. Deodhar and his deputy were present to see us off. Just when we were on the point of boarding the flight, a taxi came driving towards us and stopped. Out jumped the leader of the workers and his deputy both with 2 large garlands. The leader first garlanded Roberto and made his Namaste. Then came his deputy and did the same. Roberto was fully smothered with the garlands. He was very confused and looked at me. I told him not to remove the garlands but to do his Namaste to the 2 workers as I did. As we entered the plane, the Air hostess was staring at Roberto wondering if he was some foreign minister. In the plane itself people turned their heads to stare at him. When we were seated I told him to remove the garlands and lay them at his feet.

At the moment of drafting these memoirs I asked myself "who were the winners in this tug of war between management and labour". The answer was clear that there was neither winner nor loser. I was reminded of a BBC radio broadcast on the economic forum in which 4 panellist and the moderator were discussing the book called 'Inequality, Capital and Wealth' by Thomas Pikotee the South African economist. Pikotee had made a study of 300 years of economic data and statistics. His inclusions were that every year the rank of billionaires kept on growing. At the same time more and more young people were joining the workforce with their standard of living constantly improving. However the gap between the rich and the poor remained the same. One of the panellist suggested that the only way of bridging this gap is that more and more billionaires joined that rare species of people called Philanthropist or alternately the individual government itself should have recourse to very high doses of personal taxes on these billionaires even to the extent of 80% of personal wealth.

PART 2

As an Entrepreneur abroad

CHAPTER 8

Djibouti - A.C.C, Mumbai

A Cement Plant (in French)

The year is 1982. I have forgotten the actual date and month.
The day before I was to fly to Djibouti with Mr T V Balan,
Managing director of ACC and Mr Narayan Swamy, his
chief geologist, I stayed overnight at the ACC guesthouse at
Cuffe Parade. The transport officer woke me up at 3:00 am,
a good half an hour before scheduled time. I gulped down
a cup of tea and dressed up hurriedly. I left feeling dejected
and in low spirit because I had not shaved nor showered.
However the long drive between Cuffe Parade and the
airport was so exhilarating that I soon recovered my normal
poise and humour. Everything was still that night or rather
early morning. Nothing stirred. Not even an occasional
stray vehicle. The road was bathed in the dull glow of the
street lighting. To the right rose the majestic buildings of the
aristocrat and the rich. On the left I could hear distinctly
the lapping of the sea water and the breaking of its surf on
the stone boulders that formed the fortification of Marine
Drive. The day was breaking as we approached Haji Ali and

I could distinctly see the mosque in the middle of the sea. It was low tide and the path that led to the mosque could be clearly seen. A man was making his way on the path to the mosque for early Namaaz. How wonder I thought to begin each fresh day with the uplifting of our hearts and minds to God in prayer.

At the airport I was met by Mr Balan and Narayanswamy who told me that they were flying in a upper class and would meet me at Abu Dhabi. At Abu Dhabi we had an 8 hours stopover before taking our connecting Air Djibouti flight to Djibouti. Mr Balan approached the immigration officer asking for a visa. He stoutly refused. Balan then offered to surrender the passports and the officer grew even more angry. He opened his drawer and removed a number of passports and spread them out on the table. They were all Indian passports. At last Balan opened his beautiful leather briefcase and removed a folder which contained the agreement between Kuwait fund and the Djiboutian government concerning the funding of a feasibility report to be carried out by ACC for setting up a cement plan in Djibouti. The officer then leafed through the agreement turned to the last page studied the signatures and the seals and returned the folder to Balan. He then took our 3 passports and issued us a receipt and we came out. A taxi detached itself from a taxi stand and the driver stepped out and I thought he was Lawrence of Arabia or one of the Sheikhs from the Arab world. He wore an immaculate white flowing robe, the head gear that reached over the back and the black ring on the crown of his head. But when he was haggling with Balan about the fare I realised that he was just a common taxi driver one would find anywhere outside an international airport. With a fare agreed we drove off. The whole passage was through the desert. The road was beautifully asphalted. There was a desert breeze from the left and the taxi kept slithering away from the road, but the taxi driver expertly kept his course. We thus arrived at Ramadan hotel.

It was too late for breakfast and too early for lunch. So we settled for a brunch which was a sumptuous meal in itself. During the brunch Balan told me that I would be staying with them in a separate room in Sheraton hotel in Djibouti with lodging and expenses paid by him from his entertainment allowance. I was deliriously happy and thanked him. After the brunch there was still lot of time so we sat down in the plush sofas in the lobby. Narayanswamy the oldest of the 3 dropped his head on his chest and fell fast asleep. Soon he was snoring loudly. People moving in and out of the lobby looked at him and smiled. Being embarrassed I got up and went around to the shopping centre. There I saw Rubik cube and bought it for my daughter Geeta.

We arrived in Djibouti on schedule time and were met by an employee of the government. He said our first meeting would be next morning at 8. After settling down in the hotel the 3 of us met in the lobby and went for a stroll. Djibouti is a very small city state, most of it just a desert. During our stroll we came across a shopping centre and entered the first shop we saw. It was owned by a Gujarati who was on crutches. I bought 2 models of vintage cars in beautiful transparent boxes. As we were leaving the shop the Gujarati owner told his shop assistant to over the shop and he insisted in taking us to his house. During the drive he told us that he was involved in a head on collision with a French army truck. It was only a miracle that he escaped with his life. He said though Djibouti had received its independence many years ago the French government still maintained an army base there. Most of these French soldiers start the day by sitting on the Cafe Terrace and drinking absinthe or Schnaps a fiery alcohol. He said most of the expatriates were Gujaratis. Some were money exchangers for the Djiboutian Dinar is a freely convertible currency. Kamani's owned a coca cola bottling plant. When we reached his house he rang the bell and the Djiboutian maid opened the door. Seated in the room was his stout wife with a white and chocolate coloured earthen pot preparing butter milk with a stirrer in her hand. She added more of butter milk when she saw us. The gentleman told us if we were interested in more extensive shopping there was a supermarket called Prisunique, if we were interested eating out there was a small Vietnamese restaurant.

In the evening, we went shopping to Prisunique. It was a very big shopping centre in the form of a big shed which reminded me of a Hangar for the now defunct conquered plane. Everything was available in it, from hardware to cosmetics and foodstuff to clothing. The djiboutian government added a 30% sales tax on the imported goods. I bought a Casio VL player and a set of 6 Sony blank cassettes. I bought Opium scent of Yves and Laurent and a big kitchen knife with a Sheffield blade for my wife.

Our meeting was at 8:00 am. Present were 2 ministers, their secretaries and a female secretary went serving around tea. I was jittery and felt with stage fright since it was years that I had not done interpreting in French. Under these circumstances I learned to concentrate also on the speakers muscle movements of the mouth thus little by little my fear vanished and I was in full control.

In the evening we went to the Vietnamese restaurant for dinner. It was a small restaurant. When we entered it we were welcomed by a very old wizened woman with a bent back probably due to osteoporosis. When we sat down her assistant was also a waiter, a giant of a Vietnamese double the normal size came with a plate full of napkin drenched in very strong eau-de-cologne which we wiped our face and then back of our neck and our hands and we felt fresh. He then returned with a plate of 3 thimbles containing schnaps. We tilted our head backwards, poured the fiery liquid down our throat which created a pleasant sensation and whipped up a whopping appetite. The food was non vegetarian all prepared in an exquisite Vietnamese sauce.

At the hotel I waited till Balan and Narayanswamy had gone to their rooms. Then I quietly slipped out and went in the neighbourhood of PrisUnqiue where there were many bars. I entered the first one which was covered by a curtain. Inside there were people seated on high stools drinking and a group of girls sidled by their side. Whenever I go to a new city I am irresistibly attracted by its night life. A girl came near me and spoke in English which was all gibberish. Then she spoke French which was passable but when she spoke Italian I was delighted. She said her name was Miriam and came from Ethiopia. In olden times Ethiopia was called Abyssinia and was colonised by the Italians under Mussolini. I ordered a drink for her and myself and just as we were having it a short stocky Sicilian came and shouted "Via Via". The girls scampered like frightened rats to a side room which was covered by a curtain. The Sicilian stood there with his hands on his hips for some time. When he left the girls were all back at their posts. Miriam said that he was the boss but not a Mafia. He was quite tender hearted and owned several bars in Djibouti. When we had finished the drinks I ordered fresh drinks for both of us and said that I come with an Indian tourist group and I did not want them to miss me. On my way back I was very frightened for the streets were dimly lit. I kept on walking nonchalantly as if without fear neither looking to the right or the left. At the hotel,Balan and Narayanswamy were waiting for me. Narayanswamy told me to be very careful in this country for you could be easily mugged.

On the day before the departure I received the bad news that Balan and Narayanswamy were leaving by the earlier flight to Jeddah where they were breaking the journey to go to Yanbu where ACC were operating a cement plant. I was very upset at this news for I had not travelled alone abroad. My flight was to be 3 hours later via Aden. Balan gave me a bottle of whisky to be handed over to his secretary in Cement house. When Balan and Narayanswamy left, I rushed to PrisUnique and bought a carton of 4 Carlsberg beer and sitting in my room in the plush sofa I had all the 4 in the next 2 hours and felt very elated. The government employee picked me up and reached me in time to the airport. My flight to Aden was by a Dornier taxi flight meant only for 10 people. Among them was a Gujarati lady in sari who smiled at me and I smiled back. I dared not speak to her because of my beer fouled breath. There was no airhostess or co pilot. The door of the plane did not close. So the Pilot jumped down from the cockpit and slammed the door shut with a big blow from out. When we were airborne

I could see below the red sea and tiny specs which were ships lined up on boat size. On arrival in Aden the transit passengers had to surrender their passports. When Air India flight from Nairobi to Bombay landed at Aden our passports were returned and we were allowed to board the flight.

A few days later I left with Kalelkar Assistant geologist and Karnad the surveyor armed with his Theodoloyte for surveying the land. Their task was to collect limestone, clay and other raw materials used in the manufacture of cement and take them back to Bombay for analysis in their laboratory. It was an early morning Gulf air flight to Bahrain. The breakfast served consisted of delicious spicy Kababs. While having my breakfast, Karnad, who was affectionately called Girish by his boss Narayanswamy after the famous Kannada actor Girish Karnad, turned to me and asked me if I had a habit of pinching airline cutlery as mementos. I looked at him with an air of irritation. At Bahrain we had several hours to wait before taking the connecting flight to Djibouti. We went to the duty free liquor shop. Kalelkar bought 2 bottles of liquor for the Djiboutian ministers. On the way out both of them grabbed handfuls of plastic duty free shopping bags. I thought this to be disgusting on the part of 2 officers. I then took out the sandwiches which my wife had prepared and offered them each. While we were eating a Sudanese passenger waiting for his flight to Khartoum, remarked that we could go and have food from the counter. There we got a plate each of fried chicken, fries and bread. While we were eating the Sudanese said with surprise that coming from such a big country as India he was shocked that the travel agents were not well informed.

In Djibouti we stayed in the cheapest available hotel. I was arranging my things in my room when Karnad came to me saying that it would be better if we share the room thus halving the expenses. I said," no way I prefer my privacy more than saving a few dollars" and sent him away. In the course of the day we went to the ministry and handed over the 2 bottles of whisky. An employee told us that the jeep that would take us to the interior of Djibouti was already ready. We met the driver who was poorly dressed and there was a sharp glint in his eyes and he had a winning smile also. Suddenly I noticed that his left cheek was swollen. Thinking that it was some badly extracted tooth I asked him innocently if it hurt him. He burst into a paroxysm of laughter splattering some liquid out of his mouth. He said that it was Khat, a kind of narcotic weed which is smuggled from Ethiopia into Djibouti. Twice a week a train arrives from Addis Ababa to the port of Djibouti. The train consists of a few wooden bogies packed with people and some sitting on the roof and from all the windows the leaves of the Khat plant protruded out giving the train a festive appearance.

The road that led into the centre of Djibouti was a dirt road. As we were travelling, I saw an animal darting across the road and the driver told me that it was a Gazelle. Far away in the distance, I saw a wide expanse of water which receded and became smaller and smaller until it completely disappeared. It was the famous mirage. Having driven for another half an hour, a wild camel was hopping across the dirt road and it stopped in it track watching us. The driver accelerated the speed of the jeep and deliberately knocked it down by catching it on its hind legs. He then began to laugh madly. Looking back I saw the camel had fallen down, its hind legs twitching in pain. I asked him why he did this. He told me that by evening the camel would not be there. The tribes living in the desert would get the scent of the fallen camel, kill it and take its meat leaving the offal and other remains for the carrions. Even as he was speaking, vultures were wheeling in the sky over the fallen camel.

The place we were going to was a holiday resort consisting of individual mud huts with a small brick structure as a kitchen with tables and chairs outside for meals. It was off season. There we hired 2 more locals for the collection of the samples and stayed for 7 days. Every morning after breakfast, we took some food with us and went to the site for the collection of clay and limestone. In the evening when we sat in the open air for dinner, it was very pleasant. The desert tends to grow cool in the night. We enjoyed tremendously because Khalelkar was a good raconteur. He regaled us with stories and anecdotes from his life and that of his father who was lecturer at St Xaviers College. He told how students from the college hostel escaped at night in the neighbouring Girgaum and red light areas.

At the end of 7 days, we were back at Djibouti port. There we met Mr. Rao specialist in custom duties and had come to Djibouti to study the prevailing duties applied by neighbouring countries like Ethiopia, Eritrea, Somalia, Sudan and Aden across the red sea. He had brought along with him Noel Desouza as his interpreter. I had recommended him as the second interpreter in case of necessity.

I met Noel Desouza some years ago at Nashik. I found him to be a strange person. He said he was from Goa, from a noble patriarchal family and hence his name was spelt with a "De" and not "D'" like other commoners as me. I was sent to Nashik by Mrs. Menezes, secretary at French chamber of Commerce, saying that there were about 50 French people mostly from different ranks of the armed forces giving a demonstration of guns at the Devlali firing range. They already had 2, one was Noel Desouza and the other was a French teacher from the nearby Parsee school called Boys town. I arrived there around 8 at night and met the Chef De mission. He gave me a room at the hotel and told me to go to the conference room for my dinner. I found the place very noisy and boisterous. The 50 or so French people were all eating, drinking, chatting and laughing at the same time. This went on even after mid night. In the morning a fleet of taxis took us from the Nashik hotel to the Devlali firing range. I was put in one of the units and later on shifted on to the tank unit where the Renault engineers from the Renault motor company were showing the internal mechanism of the tank to the army jawans. I was in the tank interpreting with them. Later they took the tank for trial run through Devlali city. They told me to sit outside on the nose of the tank. I felt very proud about it thinking that people would come out and see the tank and me seated on it. Nothing happened. The people of Devlali were quite used to these daily manoeuvres of tanks. In the afternoon, we went to the officers mess for lunch. As we entered, to the right there was a table with a variety of alcoholic drinks and all the bottles were opened. In the centre was a long table with 4 or 5 large plates containing chunks of fried chicken. One night after dinner, we went to the Devlali firing range to witness firing of targets at nights by using flares. It was a most spectacular pyrotechniques that I had ever witnessed. On the last day, I was returning with 2 French men seated on the rear seat with beautiful leather bags. As we neared Nashik, the traffic grew more and more heavy. A cyclist with his friend seated on front of his seat on the bar tried to overtake on the wrong side. It came straight and crushed into our moving taxi. The cycle was thrown a few feets away tangled mass of metal. There was no sign of the 2 cyclist. I lay still in the taxi and my heart gave violent thuds. I was sure that both of them were killed or at least one. In a few seconds both of them miraculously emerged from under the vehicle and were dusting the clothes. The driver opened the door and told us to leave. A crowd had gathered around the taxi and a ruffian was trying to snatch away the French man's leather bag. I held his hand to stop him and he turned around and gave me a flat handed resounding slap on my left cheek. For the first time I saw stars during the daytime. He again went to give me another slap when I folded my hands pleadingly. Just then policemen arrived on the scene and the crowd melted away. Close on the heel of the policemen, the owner of the taxi fleet came and put the 3 of us in another taxi and sent us to the hotel. That evening there was a farewell get together in their officer's mess for the Indian officers, their wives and the French personnel. I was not able to attend it because my ear was aching me awfully and most of all I was not able to get over the humiliation of being slapped in public. So I went to the restaurant, drank well, ate voraciously and went straight to bed.

Noel in Djibouti had not changed a bit. It was his first trip abroad and he went berserk with his shopping spree. He went to PrisUnique and bought all kinds of items including 2 bottles of whisky and a big leather bag to carry all this stuff. At the airport we were 5 people ie Kalelkar, Karnad,

Rao, Noel and me. We all were to travel together to Jeddah. Noel's luggage was having excess weight and he wanted us to share his luggage. All 4 of us refused fearing carrying of drugs. Eventually Noel had to pay the excess money. At Jeddah, the 3 ACC people broke their journey to go to Yanbu where ACC was operating a cement plant. While we 2 had to pass through customs, because we were travelling by Saudi airlines. They found the 2 whisky bottles in Noel's bag and the policemen took him away with the bottles. I was very upset thinking that Noel would be doing some term in a filthy Saudi jail. But in another 10 min, I saw him returning empty handed crestfallen and with a hangdog look. He told me later that they took him to the washroom, gave him a corkscrew. He had to unscrew the bottle, pour down the drink into the sink and then dump the bottle in the garbage bin.

A few days later, I left with Nair and Subramanium, both accountants. Their task was to do the costing of the cement that would be sold in the open market. This time our itinerary was via Aden by Air India.

When we landed in Aden, we saw that Air Djibouti had just taken off and was not only gaining altitude but had become a tiny spec on the horizon. Thus our last hope of travelling to Djibouti that evening was gone. We now faced the prospect of spending the whole night in the filthy transit lounge of Aden. Nair and Subramanium viewed this situation philosophically and settled down squatting on the ground discussing office politics. As usual, I became very nervous and went looking for the duty free shops. There I found a group of very rowdy Palestinian youth making some purchases. I had always wondered whether the Palestinian youth were expelled from Aden or seeking asylum there. In one of the shops, I found a cute Panasonic solar calculator in the form of a powder compact which I bought. Then I saw the duty free liquor. I bought a bottle and going straight to the toilet, I had a big swig. I told both Nair and Subramanium from my experience in Bahrain, that we go to the counter and get our food. Once we had finished our dinner, I found that the 2 accountants were discussing the possibility of suing Air Djibouti for leaving before scheduled time. Subramanium raised a doubt that Air India landed late. In this doubt, I suggested the 2 accountants that they sue both the airlines thus their bank balances would grow. They were furious with me like a bull shown the red rag. I went to the toilet again and had another swig at the bottle. Using my bag as a pillow, I stretched myself on the dirty floor. Next morning when I got up, I had a mild hangover. We caught the morning Air Djibouti and arrived safely in Djibouti. There we took the same hotel where Kalelkar, Karnad and I were staying and went to meet the Minister. Both Nair and Subramanium, during our talk raised the topic of suing Air Djibouti. He merely smiled about it. During my stay, I found Subramanium to be very rude and offensive. One day he gave me some papers in French to be translated into English. I thrust them back into his hands saying that Interpreting and translation do not mix. Interpreting is done with a mouth and translations are done with a pen and paper. I told him to take them back to the Cement House and pass them through the usual channel.

My fourth trip was on a mission of thanks giving to the minister. It was only Balan and me. Balan stayed at Sheraton while I stayed in my cheap hotel. In the evening, we invited the minister for the dinner at Sheraton hotel. The hotel was full being some festive day in Djibouti. The minister came in his long robe made of some very costly material. He had his beard trimmed like a Goatee and in his right hand he was saying his beads. He looked indeed very majestic. During dinner I ordered a duck meat which was a speciality. I found it to be as hard as stone that even the serrated knife could not even make a dent in it and I changed it to chicken. The dessert was very special in the form of a vast variety of French cheese spread on a table tilted towards the guest. Behind, stood 3 servers. On our return to Bombay, we had a stopover at Riyadh. I had a few days visa for Saudi Arabia. This was a special bonus gift to me from ACC. I stayed at an ordinary hotel in Riyadh. After breakfast, Balan and I met and went shopping to the reputedly to the largest supermarket in the Arab world. It was indeed enormous. I concentrated only on the food section and bought 2 tins of corned beef one from Brazil and the other from Argentina. Also 2 large toblerone chocolates. As I was approaching the cashier, the muezzin sounded the call for prayer. The security people told us to leave our things as they were and hustled us out of the supermarket shutting its doors. The employees spread their mats in the direction of Mecca and fell to their knees to pray. Once their prayers were over, the supermarket opened again and I collected my things and paid for them.

Some 3 or 4 months later, Nair rang me up saying that the feasibility report was ready in English and had to be translated into French. When I went to Cement House, I saw that it was quite a voluminous job and my heart sank. But I was also glad because ACC always treated me well and did not haggle with me about the rates as though I were a fish monger. Before leaving, I went to meet Kalelkar, who was by now promoted as chief Geologist. We spoke for some time about our days in Djibouti and then he turned to me and smiled "How about a celebration". I responded naively that my wife was a good cook and they could fix any day and have a good dinner at home at my place. Kalelkar smiled back and said "D'Souza, Lets do it in style". Thus one Sunday evening, Kalelkar, Karnad and I did it in style by having our dinner at a Golden Dragon at Taj Intercontinental hotel.

Some months later, I received an early morning call from Karnad saying that Kalelkar had died of a massive heart attack in Dusseldorf, West Germany where he had been sent by ACC for some official work. I was deeply saddened and grieved at his passing away for Kalelkar was a good man and a fine human being.

CHAPTER 9

Algeria - R.C.F., Trombay

A Fertiliser Complex (in French)

From 1983 to 1985, about 45 to 50 RCF personnel were working in Annaba, Algeria operating a urea and phosphorous plant built some years previously by the French. They were also training the local Algerians in the running and maintenance of these 2 units. The RCF personnel consisted of a director and administrative staff, Engineers and technicians, and workers. All of them except the workers had their families with them and were lodged in an exclusive housing colony built for them. Their interpreter was Mr. Deodhar (a cousin of Nashik's Deodhar). Deodhar was by profession an economist from the prestigious school of Sorbonne in Paris. He spoke French fluently. Finding that being a French interpreter was more lucrative than being an economist, he joined RCF as a permanent employee.

Directors name was Mr Singh. In those early years the Indians had to face a lot of problems in their housing colony and their to and fro trips to India for holidays. Mr. Singh did not budge from his place. Hence it fell to Mr. Deodhar to seek redressal for these problems from the Algerian management. Deodhar was a good man and a conscientious worker. But fired by his zeal for his work and carried away by his own fluency in French, he upbraided the Algerian management and even criticised their lack of prompt action. When on holidays in India, Deodhars visa was cancelled and he was barred from setting foot in Algeria. The reason given by the Algerian management was that Deodhar had exceeded his brief. Even an unconditional apology to a high powered Algerian delegation to Trombay was of no avail.

During the interview I had with Debaxi, the managing director of RCF, Deodhar himself was present and gave me a written and oral test in French and okayed my selection. I was allowed to take my family with me and Mr. Pardesi of the RCF peddar road office got my wife and daughters passport on an emergency basis. While handing the passports over to me, he said that henceforth I should learn to fend for myself. Deodhar gave me a list of things to take with me among which was a bottle of whisky to be given to Mr Acharya, the new director in Algeria for use during official functions. I did carry the bottle of whisky but as a free lancer I was not convinced about the desirability of giving presents to the Director and so I kept the bottle of whisky for my own consumption.

I was glad that we were given the business class tickets of Air India flight and we left Bombay on an April morning in 1985. On arrival in Paris, we had a layover at Ritz hotel for our Air France flight to Annaba was in the morning.

After a hurried dinner, the 3 of us hired a taxi to go to Champs Elysse. I was disappointed since it was still bright daylight at 8. All the shops were closed and parishners were strolling in pairs or in groups non-chalantly and without a care in the world. My wife and daughter stopped in front of a shop window where a beautiful dress was stuck at the background with its hands spread out. It seemed to me a scare crow. For me the city of Paris was the one depicted to me in a novel of W. Somerset Maugham and Ernest Hemingway. It was the Moulin Rouge, the Latin Quarter of artists, painters, poets and people who led a Bohemian life. Arc de Triomphe could be seen far away in the distant but we were too tired to walk up to there, so we decided to return to the hotel. We took a taxi driven by a Tunisian who had been a taxi driver in Paris for only 3 months. He was not sure of the way to Ritz hotel and we went astray. For a moment I felt that he was trying to waylay us in some quite spot. Then seeing a girl passed that way he asked her the direction but instead of replying she opened the door next to the driver and sat inside and directed him straight to Ritz hotel. I found that fare was even less than what I had paid while I was coming. The next morning the 3 of us were seated in the dining room for breakfast. A fat maid seeing my wife's sari ignored us. She served some 3 Japanese businessmen who had come after us. As she was passing I asked her in polite French why she is ignoring us. She was all flustered and she came back soon with 3 plates of porridge. During our flight to Annaba by Airfrance we found a **purser** to be a great admirer of Indians. He said that once every 2 years he goes to Southern India to an ashram for doing yoga and meditation. So plied my wife and me with Champagne several times.

On arrival in Annaba we were met by Chandra Moily the travel officer and Deo the accountant. They put our luggage in the imported Suzuki van and drove us to the RCF housing colony. There we found that the houses were all prefabricated Canadian houses. Our house all were 3 bedrooms and a kitchen which extended into a sitting room which also served as the dining room. In the washroom there was a large tub filled with water and also 2 jerry cans filled with water. At the entrance to the bathroom was a small cubical which was a toilet. It was horrible filthy left like that by the Bachelor Indians who stayed there previously. There were no cupboards so we used one bedroom to keep our clothes.

In the evening V.K.Singh, an Engineer came to fetch us and took us to meet Acharya, the director. He and his shy and timid wife were talking to us when a rat ran round the house. Acharya said they were his pets. He told me to assemble in front of his house at 8 in the morning. Besides Acharya who drove the Suzuki van there was Chandra Moily, Deo, Krishnan, Dr.Dutta and I. Krishnan was a huge bodied man with a very broad naam across his forehead. He was a computer specialist and worked in his own special room. Dr Dutta was a Ph.d in Chemistry and worked in the lab. He also knew a smattering of French and therefore voluntarily agreed to be demoted in designation from lab technician to interpreter in French. Thus getting the chance of travelling with his family abroad. The drive to the factory which lasted 40 minutes was fantastic. The road was absolutely smooth and asphalted. Imported French Peugeot cars flew past at breakneck speed. The Casualty rate in road accident and being crippled early in life is very high in Algeria. At the factory we had an administrative office to ourselves. Within this there was a cabin for Mr.Acharya alone. Outside, the space was shared by 4 of us i.e. Chandra Moily, Deo, Dr Dutta and me. At 9 o clock Chandra Moily got up and stuffing his briefcase with passports, tickets and other documents took the key of the van from Acharya, left for his daily trip to the Immigration Office and travel agencies. At 10 o clock Acharya put on his white helmet and went for his one hour inspection tour of the 2 units. Chandra Moily came back at 1 and kept his briefcase on the table and sitting on his chair, he spread out his legs and heaved a high sigh of relief. After sometime he opened the briefcase, removed the passports and tickets and opening his drawer, he flung them inside and shut the drawer with a bang. Then he looked round at all of us as if to say "Any Comments". Deo was a huge bodied man on two small legs. He lumbered like a bear and when he worked he bent his head on one side and traced his letters and figures like a child in a kindergarten school. One day the chief Algerian accountant came with a stack of papers and dumped them on Deo's table and turning towards us he said "Your accountant has closed the accounts to the nearest digit instead of making the figures tally" and then stormed out angrily. All the while Dr Dutta kept on translating some document while his mouth moved as if chewing some Bengali herbal gum. I was given a document to be translated into French from English.

At 1, we had our tiffin, each one in his own seat. 20 minutes later, the engineers started coming to gather around Acharya. The first one was Tandon. The others varied from day to day. They chatted like schoolboys and this reached the peak when any officers had returned from India from the holidays. He would narrate every small incident that took place during the journey.

Thursdays and Fridays were holidays and Thursday was the day when we went to main market for shopping. Those who had the use of Suzuki van would take their own families and any friend they fancied with their families. The rest of us travelled by a Tata trailer which had only a few seats along the side and a few would stand supporting ourselves from the top. The market was quite near to the factory. It was a very large market well divided into different sections. There were the grains and cereals, vegetables, fish, meat, clothing and toys. All the goods were shoddy and of inferior quality with no much variety and always in short supply and all imported from China and East European countries. Eggs were imported from Holland and always in short supply. Meat consisted of chicken and horse meat. The rule of thumb to guide us was to see where a queue was forming, join the queue first and asks questions later, thus I once joined a queue and when I reached at the counter I found gunny bags full of peanuts. I bought 100 grams. The most favourite sections were the clothing and draperies for ladies. They bought pillow cases, bed sheets and even lacework. The dinars were spent freely because they were of new use in India. Children delighted in visiting the toy shop but unfortunately very rarely new stocks of toys would be there from China. After shopping we went to the Independent Square which was actually rectangular shaped and not a Square. There we sat on the benches with eating meat pattice and ice creams. We watched the Algerian children playing. Algerians had very large families. Their children had angelic faces but when they played they were little devils. They would beat up a younger brother or a sister kicking them on the shins.

Social life was strictly on the system of rank and office. The Engineers and the administrative staff occupied the quarters in the central park and they intermingled only amongst themselves. The technicians among whom I was included mixed only with other technicians. We often went for walk with our neighbours the Surves. The workers were confined in their own quarters being without families.

At this stage, I came to know that I was employed on the salary of a worker because I was an outsider and a free lancer. I brought this to the notice of Mr Acharya who promised that when he went to India on holidays he would bring the matter to the notice of the management. In the meanwhile, Deo came on Friday to my house with a stack of documents to be translated. I told him that as a worker I was not allowed to do over time. Another day V.K. Singh came to me requesting if my daughter could take some classes organised for the children of the officers. I replied that he should be ashamed of himself to ask a workers daughter to teach officers children. When Acharya came back from his holidays, I met him. Suddenly his whole features were transformed. He was extremely agitated, looked like a man who was battered and bruised as he told me that the management gave him a dressing down telling him not to interfere into the matters of management. It was such a frightful experience that he would never attempt it again. However, he managed to get me my normal officers salary but without retrospective effect. This only goes to prove that the PSU employs people on temporary basis on lower salary even when they are more qualified than the permanent hands and when treating their own officers shows utter ruthlessness.

On a Diwali day, there was a get together in the community hall and Mr. Harohalli, who was an actor in his own right and claimed to be member of Dr. Shreeram Lagoos troupe, was in charge of organising the entertainment. It was a good show. There was singing and dancing on the part of the children, a skit and a housie.

The day of obligation for Catholics was Friday. Mr Lal an Engineer was kind enough to give us a lift to the church of St Augustine for mass. The church is situated on the top of a high hill and is visible for miles around from Annaba. St Augustine famous for his Confessions was bishop of Annaba at the end of the fourth century. Annaba was then known as Hippo. Under the French, Annaba came to be known as Bone and under Islam it got its present name.

There was a rumour that Mr Debaxi the managing director of RCF was visiting Annaba. I was not aware when he came, where he stayed and when he left. All I knew was there was a big dinner for him in one of the Officers quarters.

One day a picnic was arranged to the borders of Tunisia. Once again Mr Lal was good enough to take me and my family in his Suzuki van. The drive to the Tunisian border lasted for 2 hours, was one of the most unforgettable and beautiful countryside. The picnic itself was in a Eucalyptus grove which reminded me of the picnic in Nashik. My wife had baked a chicken for the occasion and Lals family and mine had a good time. Those who could not attend the picnic were many and they were those without the Suzuki van and the workers. A special mention must be made of Raju. He lived along with the workers for he had left his family behind in Kerala. He was a Chemistry graduate and trained Algerians in the lab. In his free time he practised

Homeopathy. When he came from India, he brought with him an array of homeopathic pills and powders and opened a free clinic in his workers quarters. The very poor and the marginalised Algerians living in the hovels outside our colony came to Raju for treatment which was free. I remember seeing once a very old lady in torn clothes wearing a scarf round her head and her neck with feet wrapped in dirty rags and tied by a string hobbling towards Raju's quarters for treatment.

At the end of 1 year, Acharya asked me if I could carry on for another year. I turned down the offer because my daughter had only 1 years leave from her college. The day we left in the morning, Mr Acharya, his wife and V K Singh came to our house to see us off and Chandra Moily was there to take us to the airport. On arrival at Charles Degor airport in Paris, we left our unwanted luggage at the left luggage section and broke our journey for a 2 weeks trip of Europe. We took a night train at Gar Du Nord and arrived in the morning at Lourdes. In the evening we went to Rome and from there to Florence, Venice and across the English Channel to spend 4 days in London and then back to Paris again to spend another 4 days there before we took the return flight to India.

The RCF people who worked in Annaba had earned and saved enough money to buy flats in Vashi and other townships in the newly burgeoning Navi Mumbai. One man who to my knowledge took advantage of staying so close to Europe as to take his family for a trip around Europe was Godbole. He was very resourceful and enterprising and friendly person who worked as a Lab tech both in RCF and Annaba.

CHAPTER 10

Algeria revisited -Star Industrial Textile Industries, Mumbai

A Textile Factory

This is one of those jobs that should never have been. From 1987 to 1989 I went through a very lean period where interpreting was concerned. While on the other hand where translations were concerned I was swamped by them. The reasons for this are not far to seek. In the first place I knew 2 female Italian interpreters at Raymonds who said that they did interpreting only as a hobby and looked down upon translations as a nuisance. For me it was food on the table for the whole family. Then from among those who also do translations besides interpreting, they do only one language either Italian or French. My translations which included Italian and French also extended to German, Spanish and Portuguese. Furthermore I paid supreme importance to the accuracy in my translations and here I disposed of 3 technical dictionaries of which one was trilingual. My translations were neatly tied with double spacing and on a high quality bond paper. Also I saw that my work was done speedily and expeditiously. Then I stuck to the delivery schedule with a religious fanaticism. For this I made use of courier and fax shops that were around Thane station. I did all kinds of translations jobs from the single page commercial correspondence, technical documentation, operating manual, confidential bank reports for Standard Chartered Bank and advertising material with proof reading for Lintas. Besides a lot of miscellaneous jobs for private translation agencies like ABC translation agency and Oriental Languages Bureau. All this came at a very heavy price. I was weary in body and listless in mind and my nerves were on edge. So I started drinking. Under these circumstances I was contacted by Pahuja of Star Industrial and Textile Industries, Dhanraj Mahal, Apollo Bhunder Road. He told me that they had a textile factory project coming up at Tissemsilt, Algeria. They wanted a good French interpreter at the earliest. The very idea of being separated from my family for 3 months and going to a God forsaken country like Algeria made my heart sink. My wife and daughter told me that I should at least go and see what it is all about without committing myself to anything. I met Pahuja and the terms the company offered were very magnanimous and irresistible. Still I baulked. I asked Pahuja to give me an hour's time for reflection.

I went to the Gateway of India and looked at the vast sea. I saw the small fishing crafts bobbing up and down in the gentle roll of the sea. In the distance I could hear the chugging of a Moto launch and then I saw it full of tourist going to visit the Elephanta Caves. I then turned and walked straight passed Regal Cinema to Leopold Cafe where I ordered my favourite beer Khajurao which was also the strongest and gulping it down I felt good. I returned to Star office and accepted Pahuja's offer.

The day I was to leave for Algeria I started drinking in the afternoon. By evening when I went to the airport with my wife, daughter and Brother-in-law, I was high. At the airport Star's transport officer gave me my passport, ticket and foreign exchange. At the same time he introduced me to 2 technicians from Themist company in Pune, who were going to Tissemsilt for some affluent treatment plant. This indeed was an extraordinary providence. Both took charge of me immediately, helped me to go through all the clearances and get my boarding pass. When we were inside they went around seeing the shops and I went to the duty free liquor shop, bought a bottle of whisky, went to the toilet and had a swig. After that everything was a blur. The Swiss Air security man came to me in the plane asking me my boarding pass which I had lost by then. My next memory is that of my seating down in the transit lawn of Zurich airport. When my 2 companions were away I went to the toilet and had another swig. After that I dimly remember the immigration officer at Algiers stamping my passport. Next I remember at Tissemsilt my 2 companions held me as I was about to fall in the ditch. There Mr Iyer, Star's secretary at Tissemsilt took charge of me. Before leaving one of the Engineers gave me a shawl because it was cold. Mr Iyer took me to a large shed at one end of which a man was lying asleep and I was told to occupy the bed at the other end. Mr. Iyer helped me to remove my shoes and to put away my passport, ticket and foreign exchange in suitcase and locking it gave me the key. In the morning he took me in for breakfast in a shed which was leaking because of the melting snow. Vilas the cook and a stout Algerian woman who helped him came to see me. After breakfast Iyer told me to take my passport and ticket and come to his office. By then I had already planned to bolt from there. All I needed was my passport. I could buy a ticket with the foreign exchange had. But I had to surrender both passport and ticket. I gave them to him but at the last moment I pounced upon him to take the passport back. By then he had opened his drawer and keeping them both inside locked it. He told me with a smile that the 3 months would pass swiftly in the best of company and that there was nothing to fear. He then took me to an adjacent room where an Algerian translator was working and he gave me some translation work. When Iyer had left I asked the Algerian where I could buy a packet of cigarettes. He volunteered himself and came back with a packet of French cigarette called Gauloises, the worlds best known chest breakers. I lit one cigarette and walking up and down outside the room I was smoking, when an Indian by name Jawle came and spoke to me. Surprisingly he too was from Thane but he was lucky for he had bargained hard with the Star people because of his specialised job and had his family with him. That afternoon for lunch we had chicken stew in a large bowl with bread. Fridays and Mondays were chicken days. After lunch Mr Iyer took me to meet Gurumurthy Star's director at Tissemsilt. He was a very kind and affable man. He told me at that very moment that his daughter was getting married at Hyderabad and here he was slogging here like a slave at work for such are the vicissitudes of life. He said that there are various ways of passing my evening there. In one of the houses, 2 people sang Bhajans. In another house some cooked Indian food on a spirit lamp and chatted and made merry. I went to the house where the Bhajans were being sung. There were only 2 people and I could hardly sit still in my chair. I fidgeted all the time and abruptly I could stand it no longer; I got up and walked away.

In the room, where they were doing Indian cooking, I met my 2 friends from Pune. I went to a 3rd room where the man was lying on bed reading some magazine. His name was Bindra. I spent at least more than an hour talking pleasantly.

The next morning, Iyer told me to help Mr Nath, a textile professor who was taking some classes for trainees. Mr Nath told me to sit in a chair and help him where his French was wrong. Instead, I found that the trainees were looking at me and whispering all the time. So I took Nath's leave and left. By now, I asked Nath where I could buy a bottle of wine. In the evening both of us set out for the place and there I bought a bottle of wine. Some days later, Iyer told me that I should accompany Mr Rao. He was an elderly man who was a legal consultant. I had to go with him to a court which was one of the arbitration rather than legal binding. An Algerian worker had been dismissed and he had appealed to this court. The hearing was on that day. When we entered the court, we found in front a single judge seating in front of the table and a woman standing in front of him screaming at the top of her voice and waving her fist under the very nerves of the judge. Rao and I sat on a bench and every now and then the people sitting there broke into hilarious laughter at the hysterical shouting of the woman. I asked one of my neighbour & he said that her husband had divorced her by uttering 3 talats. The judge fed up finally adjourned the case and ours did not come up for hearing.

Another day, I was told to go with Mr Rao to the doctor. The clinic was on the ground floor in a dilapidated building. Inside a doctor was seated alone at the table with another chair by his side but no bed for examination. On the table, he had spread neatly his stethoscope, syphgo manometer etc. He made Rao sit in the chair and asked him a lot of pertinent questions in French which I translated. Then he carried out a thorough examination of Mr Rao taking his pulse, his blood pressure, feeling his reflexes by tapping with a mallet. Then he sat still for a long time reflecting. Suddenly he opened his drawer and removed a small book called the Pharmacopia. He went through it and prescribed 3 different medicines. I could never forget this visit because I wondered all the time if the doctor was going through his oath of Hyppocrates like a mantra to remind him of his duty to help the sick.

On Christmas day, I was having a wash when Gurumurthy came to my shed to wish me. I always wondered how a man with such onerous duties could find the time to wish me. He said that in the evening there will be a small get together in Mr Iyer's office. Besides me there was only another Christian. Mr Iyer gave a glass of beer with pastries.

In the meanwhile, my cash was over. So I borrowed some dinars from Nath and he was only too glad to oblige provided when I returned to India and I send a cheque to his wife for Dinars are no use in India. Later when I needed more money, I borrowed from Iyer and he was also too glad provided I paid his married sister living in Kalyan in cash.

One day Nath took me to the site. All the textile missionary had been installed but the civil works and the masonry were not completed. These jobs came under a Delhi based company and the Sikhs from Punjab, Haryana and New Delhi were crawling all over the factory hammering, riveting and banging the roof and the masonry in place. Then we went to the office of these contractors. There were 3 officers inside. 2 days later, I visited their office and asked one of their officers if he could dial my home number. I was paying him money in Dinar but he waived it aside. I was surprised when my house phone was ringing. My wife came on the line and I told her in Konkani to send me a telegram saying that my mother is in ICU with a heart attack. Next morning Mr Gurumurthy called me and showed me the telegram. I pretended to be shocked and even feigned some crocodile tears. He immediately called Iyer and told him to contact head office in Algiers to book my ticket at the earliest. That afternoon itself, I was packing up and the Algerian lady came to wish me. I gave her the big cake of sandalwood soaps and a tube of Colgate toothpaste. She was only too happy to receive them. I left by the afternoon bus to Algiers and for the first time I travelled 2 hours of journey fully awake and enjoyed the beautiful Algerian countryside. I stayed at the head office for 2 days and in the evening, I used to go out with the cook to the market. I saw all around 2 floor buildings with corridor running right round them and clothes hanging around for drying. This blocked all the light entering the houses.

When I went to the airport, I met the Delhi contractor with 5 Sikhs. He told me to keep an eye on them for they could only speak Hindi and Punjabi. Once my boarding pass was in hand, I saw an opened bar and people drinking draught beer. The only condition that was one should pay in dollars. I offered the 5 Sikhs but they refused. I had 2 draught beers and thus I arrived at Zurich airport. There I had to take the connecting Swiss Air flight to Bombay. The 5 Sikhs were allowed to board the plane but I was stopped. The security man looked me up and down. I was wearing a good pant made from top Raymond suiting and a shirt made from Bombay Dyeing shirting. I wore a natty tie and my shoes were well polished. The officer told me that there is no place in the economy class and asked the Air Hostess to take me to the First class. There I was given a seat next to a fat Swiss German lady who gave me one look and then looked away. When I was seated I spoke to her few words in German and she was very pleased. Knowing that I had a daughter, she rummaged in her bag and gave me a military watch made of Khaki and Blue camouflage cloth. She said,"It is just a toy but it is a Swiss watch and gives perfect time". When the trolley came with whisky and Caviar, I was delighted. Having had enough for my satisfaction, I felt fast asleep and woke up only in Bombay. When I turned to the Swiss lady, she gave me a stern and grave look of disapproval.

I was delayed at the money changers and when I came out the 5 Sikhs were waiting for me. I said I had arrived at my home. Then one of them asked me if I could give them some Rupees. I gave a 100 rupee note.

A year later, Iyer rang me up from Dhanraj Mahal that they had a long telex in French to be translated. When I went to Star's office, I was ushered into Mr Gurumurthy's office. He gave me a broad smile and showed me the telex in French and its translation in a very small note. I said that this is not the translation but a précis writing. It took me more than an hour to do the complete translation of the whole telex and Mr Gurumurthy remarked "Your translation is a real wonder but your interpreting at Tissemsilt was a near disaster; he said what is the secret of your translation". I said that first you should know the foreign language very well. Secondly you should not leave out a single sentence. Thirdly you should understand what the writer intends to say rather than what he says. Fourthly you should write it in good English not just grammatically correct but with style. I submitted my bill and within half an hour I was paid my cheque.

CHAPTER 11

Italy-M/s. Stefano
Stefani, Vicenza

Diamond studded jewellery
manufacturing works (in Italian)

Mr Suresh Mehta was a prosperous diamond merchant with office in Opera house in Bombay and the Jewellers shop in Coimbatore. In 1992, he bought a unit in the Gem and Jewellery Complex in SEEPZ Andheri, with the objective of manufacturing 18 carat diamonds studded gold rings with 100% to be exported to USA. This was to be with the collaboration of Stefano Stefani Vicenza Italy who would supply them with the Gold melting furnace, machines and other toolings necessary for the trade. It also included the 3 months training for Suresh Mehta's 3 boys, as he called them, in Stefano's works in Vicenza. Mr Suresh Mehta asked me if I could speak Hindi. I replied that I could speak as well as any person you would come across on the streets of Bombay or Thane. The 3 boys names were Subash, Khitish and Ramesh. They were expert craftsmen in the designing of gold jewellery. Subash and Khitish were from Bengal and Ramesh was from Madras. Except for Hindi and their own regional languages, they could not speak English. Ramesh managed with a little smattering of English. On the day we were to leave, Suresh Mehta's son also came to the airport to help us. The 3 boys were as excited as school boys about to go on their first school picnic but the immigration authorities returned the 3 passports because they were not stamped with no objection as required for non graduates. After considerable wrangling between Suresh Mehta's son and the officer in charge the matter was finally settled to the mutual benefit and satisfaction to both parties in the way that is known to us Indians.

Suresh Mehta was a member of Lufthansa club and said he was travelling first class and would meet us at Frankfurt airport. When we arrived there, he tried to 'smuggle' me into the Lufthansa club cafeteria but the old sharp eyed German woman saw this and gave a shout to Suresh Mehta. He was known to her very well. She ordered both of us to get out. Suresh Mehta then said that he was breaking his journey in Frankfurt for he had some business there and he would meet us next day at Vicenza. During our stop over at the transit lounge, I asked the 3 boys if they were given any foreign exchange or additional emoluments besides the pay for the 3 months and they all said no. The only thing that they were all excited about was going abroad. Our Alitalia flight to Venice from Frankfurt arrived in time. I told the 3 boys to queue up before me. There was a quite a long queue for immigration and customs check. When our turn came, I stepped forward and told the immigration officers in Italian that these boys were going to Vicenza for training and I was their interpreter. He took our 4 passports and then removing a big book from the drawer, he went through it laboriously and carefully until he found what he was looking for. In the meanwhile, the Italians behind standing in the queue were fretting and fuming. After checking thoroughly, our passports were stamped and returned to us and we had to move to the customs check. The customs officer asked us to open all our bags. He saw 2 big bags and asked what they contained. I translated and Subash replied that one contained rice and the other contained Farsan "Sweets" brought from the American dry fruit store at Flora fountain. The custom officer asked that (haven't you brought any sugar for there is a shortage of sugar in Italy). The Italians in the queue started laughing. The custom officer went in and came back after some time with 2 huge sniffer dogs. They went carefully through our open bags and 2 large bags several times. Finally satisfied, the custom officer told us to close our bags. When we went out Mr. Stefano himself was at the exit. He was a tall and huge man wearing spectacles which were tied behind his neck with a chord. In his hand, he had an umbrella. Behind him was Piero his assistant. Our luggage was put in the 2 cars and we drove through Venice to Vicenza. It was winter time and so it was dark at 6 pm. Lights twinkled from the buildings and offices around us. The red parking lights of the cars ahead of us came on and off and all the while there was a slight drizzle. All the way, Stefano told me that Mr Suresh Mehta had rented 2 apartments for us. One was near the factory with a few minutes walk and the other quire far away. Stefano suggested that we all stayed together in the flat near the factory. When we arrived there, we took the lift to the 2nd floor. Stefano opened the flat and we entered a small one bedroom hall flat. The bedroom had a double bed and Stefano told me and Khitish to occupy the bed whereas Subash and Ramesh to sleep at the sofa cum beds in the sitting room. He took me to the window and showed me the small super market. It was called supermarket Car. He said that we could get all our food items there. He asked me, if I had any money. I said not for official use. So he called Mehta a big miser and gave me a 10000 lira note for expenses.

As soon as Stefano left the boys put on the t.v. & kept on switching channels until they came across the channel called Colpogrosso. This programme was one of talent contest but the girls were scantily clad. So we all stopped to watch it. I told Subhash that we go to the supermarket Car to buy some chicken so that he can start cooking. When we both left the other 2 boys also followed us. The supermarket was very small one but had enough varieties of food stuff. Subhash got 2 trays, one of chicken breast & another of chicken lollypops. I personally took 100 grams of fine sliced ham. Once we were back in our flat I told Subhash that I am going for a stroll & went to the end of supermarket Car where there was a bar. I entered it. There was a big boystrous crowd of Italians. I sat at a table & ordered Birra Perroni. Here I was I thought to myself, in Italy, in an Italian bar, amidst Italians & drinking an Italian beer. What more could one expect in life!

Next morning at 8 Piero came to fetch us. We took only a few minutes to reach the Works. Strangely it was in a residential area, a one floor structure. Piero rang the bell & a tall smart man with the professorial look opened the door. This was Roberto, the man in charge of melting the gold & preparing the rough 18 carats gold rings. At the entrance we had to stand a few seconds on the vibrating mat meant to remove the dust. Then we were each given blue overall. We were taken to the room on the left where about 25 to 30 polishing girls were seated engaged in grinding & polishing the rough rings. They were 5 in a row each with a overhead reading lamp in level with the face. On the table there were 4 trays,the first contained the rough rings, the second contained polished rings, the third contained the toolings including a small grinding wheel,a brush, pincers, etc. The fourth contained the dust. A table was kept against the wall with 4 chairs. This was in front of the polishers. So we sat with our back to the girls and Piero brought 3 books containing different designs of rings. He gave them to each of the boys along with some soft gum like material for preparing the moulds of the rings. I sat there for quiet sometime watching the 3 boys working. Then I got up stretched my legs and walked back towards the rows of working girls. One girl was chewing a chewing gum looked up at me & smiled. She asked me what my name was, I said it was D'Souza. No your complete name. I said it was "Bonaventure Emanuel D'Souza". She replied smiling that her name was "Manuela". By the side of the wall there was a cassette player & Enzo Ramazotti's cassette was being played. He was a popular singer from Rome. I continued on my way & across at right angles to the polishing room was the furnace room & Roberto was working there. I crossed this & came to the dining room which had a few chairs, a fridge & a coffee vending machine. I went to the next room parallel to this which was the diamond setting room. Piero was seated last alone for he was the supervisor. Above him there was a big calendar of Nudes. I was staring at it when he said take your pick. Here all were men except 2 elderly women. One of them spoke to me in the venetian dialect. She had a look of a Peasant. I could hardly follow her. Before lunch a middle aged polishing woman called "Nonna"(grand mother) for our afternoon food. No one was allowed to go out for food nor any food was allowed to be brought in. During lunch break there was much mingling & Khitish went towards a petiet & demeure girl called Sabrina to practise a few of the Italian words he had learnt from me on her. She rebuffed him angrily saying in German "gehen Sie Weg"(go away). I was surprised at this. When they were all back at table working, I went to Sabrina & said, "Sprechen Sie Deutsch" (do you speak German). She looked at me surprised. She said she came from Bolzano a city about 60 kilometers from Vicenza where she said the people are bilingual. They speak both German & Italian from time immemorial. She didn't know the origin of this. She said she stayed at an aunt's place in Vicenza during the week & went to Bolzano on Saturdays & Sundays to her parents house.

In the afternoon Suresh Mehta turned up & went straight to the first floor to meet Stefano. Here Stefano & the other Secretarial staff had their offices. After an hour or so he came down & told me we will go to the bank to change money. On the way he told me to bring my own foreign exchange & henceforth I should pay for my own food. I looked at him angrily & said tomorrow you will ask me to pay the rent. He then looked away & laughed. On the way he asked me about my bank balance, whether I earned enough to make a living & when once his unit in the Gem & Jewellery Complex In Seepz was ready he would give me a job as a Supervisor. I looked at him & said "thank you very much. I would never exchange the romance & thrills of working as a free lancer to the boredom & a drudgery of a 9 a.m. to 5 p.m. white collar worker". After we changed the money we went further to Suburbs to a big shop called Ramona where woollen clothings were sold. While he was purchasing some woollen clothes I went to a slot machine & for the first time in my life I managed to get a bar of chocolate from it. On our way back he lost his way & told me roughly how do we go back. I told him I am not your guide,you better stop & find the way. However we finally managed to reach Stefano's factory. He said that I should meet him at 8 next morning at his hotel to help him while he left. I was there at 8. He told me to carry his Suitcase. Instead I went to bell boy & asked him to help the Gentleman to lift the Suitcase. When we reached Vicenza station the Porter came & I told him to wait there till the train for Milan arrived & help the gentleman in it. On my return journey I took a bus from Vicenza. It was crowded with school children. All the windows were shut because of the fear of "Corrente" i.e. is the draught. The inside of the bus the smell was terrible. There was the musty smell of woollen clothings not washed for ages & body odours from bodies that had not seen water for a week.

Saturdays & Sundays were holidays. On Saturday we went for a walk & came to the Cosmetic Shop. We entered it. Subhash took a nail polish,he opened it & took it to his nose to smell it. The sales girl all scarlet with rage came rushing to Subhash. I slipped out to let him face the music. When we came out we saw in the distance snow capped hills & mountains. The 3 boys said that since we had a whole day to ourselves we could walk up to the mountains to play with the snow. Instead I suggested we take a bus & go to the place which was called Asiago. We reached there after 2 hours & we found that the snow capped hills & mountains were no nearer than at Vicenza. There we found some patches of snow & the boys started making snow balls & throwing at one another. Then tiring of this sport we went to the near by ice skating ring. We were turned away saying it was only for members. The next morning being Sunday I said I was going for mass. They could accompany me or stay back. They preferred to come with me. After the service we came out & saw on the opposite side at some distance a newsstand. At the top there were some pornographic magazines. But they were all covered in Cellophane covers & cellotape.

On Monday Roberto called us saying that he was executing big order of gold rings for USA. And so the 3 boys & myself had to enter the furnace room to watch the demonstration. Before starting he told us that what he is about to show is top secret. I said that I had to note everything in the diary given by Mr Suresh Mehta. After some reflection he said there was no objection to that. The whole production lasted about 3 hours. I had the unenviable task of doing 2 jobs at the same time. On the one hand I had to explain everything to the boys in Hindi & on the other I had to jot down everything in English in the diary.

Being tired of finding ourselves every night after dinner cooped up in the flat we decided to go in search of Jenny. But the city was all dead. So we went to the railway station which was equally dead. There was no rush of people going in & out of the station. Suddenly I saw across in the park a shadowy figure moving up & down. We went towards it, to our horror it was a transvestite. So we rushed back to the safety of road & returned to our place. Vicenza is not Rome.

One day Stefano (the Diamond setter & not the Boss) arranged for a Disco party. 3 or 4 girls along with Stefano & the 4 of us went to the disco place. It was in an open air & in the centre was raised platform where the dancers were dancing. The 3 boys were soon lost in the crowd. I was seated by the side in a chair & finally I managed to find Subhash. He had bent his knees. His body was all twisted & contorted & his hands were flaying the air. He was really enjoying himself. I went to buy a glass of beer but its price was exorbitant so I gave up the idea. Another day the same Stefano arranged a Pizza party at an Neapolitan Pizzeria. It was a same group that went there. The Pizza was really exquisite & the beer was cheap. So Stefano & I had a glass of beer each.

On Valentines Day Khitish told me to get some flowers for Sabrina. So I went out. Going out & coming in was a problem. Roberto was in charge of opening the door & he was not happy about this job. Somehow I managed to go out & bought a good Bouquet of Flowers at moderate rates. When I returned, Roberto opened his eyes wide when he saw me with flowers. I said they were for Khitish. After lunch break he offered it to Sabrina. This time she accepted the flowers gracefully & allowed him a peck on her cheek.

Alfredo was a consultant. Twice a month he visited Stefano's & went from person to person enquiring if they had any problems & help it resolving them. He stopped next to me & saw that we were of the same height. He said he was having a 3 piece woollen suit which couldn't fit him any longer because of his expanding girt. When he brought it after some days I found it to be excellent 3 piece suit made of chocolate brown heavy wool & Madras check pattern. It fitted me to a T. I was very proud of my free acquisition.

For Easter Vacations Stefano told me that we should not stay back in our flat but go to Venice,Verona,Padua & if possible even Rome. I asked him for the money. He said that there was no problem & he would give me enough lire to Suresh Mehta's account. So on Thursday we left for Venice. The train journey was short. We found that the motor launches were very expensive so we preferred to walk along the Grand Canal. We thus came to St. Marks Cathedral. There several urchins with bags slung across the shoulder & holding large cones of grains surrounded us. Each of us brought a cone & then we started scattering the grains in the piazza & watched as the pigeons came swooping down to eat the grains & leave in a flurry afterwards. After this we went to the several shops on the side of the Piazza where small & large glass items blown at the near by Murano Glass Works being sold. We could only admire them without buying for they were too costly.

On Saturday before Easter we caught a night train to Rome at Vicenza. The train was full without being crowded. We walked along the corridor & all the compartments were closed. Finally we found a compartment which was closed from inside. We banged on the door until a sleepy eyed Sengelaese opened the door & began speaking in French. While I was arguing with him the 3 boys made a brilliant tour –de-force & jumped into the 3 vacant berths & pretended to be fast asleep. Thus I was left alone in the corridor. When the Sengelaese had gone to his berth I was left alone in the corridor. I walked up & down the corridor whole night watching the stations fly past at the lights of the cities. In my hand I had a small flat aluminium snuff box. I opened it till the holes corresponded & tapped out a little snuff in my hand & thus sniffing it & managed to pass the night.

In the morning when we arrived at Rome terminal there were 3 or 4 tarts at the exit. The boys made straight for them to make fun of them. I told them to be careful as these women are vicious & are even capable of kicking you with their high heeled shoes on your shins. I managed to find a 'pensione',the cheapest lodging available in Italy. I gave the card of the pensione to the boys & told them to go to the Vatican. From the store below the pensione I bought a small bottle of wine & with some sandwiches I had my breakfast & went to sleep. At 3 p.m. the boys were back & I said I would go now to the Vatican. They insisted coming along with me again. At the Vatican the Piazza was almost empty after the afternoon ceremonies. I went into the Vatican straight to the first chapel on the right. There was a famous Pieta of Michael Angelo. I stood in front of this chapel & it reminded me of the sixth of the seven sorrows that pierced our ladys heart during her sojourn on earth. It is the bringing down of the dead body of Christ from the cross & laying it in his Mothers arms. The face of Mary contemplating her dead son's face & the right hand of Christ limp by his side bring out clearly the grief of Mary & the death of her son. From there I walked straight up to the main Altar. There on level with my mouth to the right lies the bronze statue of St. Peter. I kissed his feet which millions of pilgrims down the centuries kissing those feet have made the feet so smooth it seems that St. Peter was stricken from leprosy.

Towards the end of my contract one of the diamond setters who came from Padua said that if I came on Sunday morning he would show me Padua. However none of the boys should come with me & that was his condition. At Padua I met him along with his girl friend at the Station & he took me around the old city with his cobbled pavements then to the Stadium where the football match was going on with much cheering & booing & then to the Cathedral of St. Anthony of Padua. Outside the Cathedral there were Pullman buses from Germany that had brought German Pilgrims. After visiting the different chapels inside when I came out I went straight to a girl who was selling mementos. I was attracted to her not because she was beautiful but she was dressed poorly but neatly & had an extraordinary aura of resignation & holiness. I brought a small wooden memento for my house.

At the end of 3 months I went to Stefano asking him to return my passport & ticket as I was in no mood to stay any longer. He said that he can do only if Suresh Mehta allowed him. The next day he said that Suresh Mehta wanted me to stay a month longer. I asked him if there was any talk of any extra foreign exchange & rupees. That topic was not raised at all. Hence I said that I am not interested in staying. I booked my next flight back to Venice & Bombay via Frankfurt. Ramesh accompanied me to the airport in the bus that left Vicenza. At Venice I took Alitalia flight to Frankfurt. There I took the connecting Lufthansa flight to Bombay. While returning from the toilet on the Frankfort Bombay sector I heard a familiar female voice calling my name. I looked back It was Mrs. Sunita Kapur who with Rene Kapur her husband owned a group of Burlington's Group of Companies. They exported readymade garment specially boxers & t-shirts to coin & la Renascente 2 well known chains of supermarkets in Italy. For the last several years I was called at least more than twice a year to Burlington's factory in Thane for interpreting in Italian when some top officers from these 2 Italian companies came to discuss new designs,fashions, prices, etc. Few months later I was going to the Times Of India, when I saw obituary column in memory of Mrs Sunita Kapur nee Mulgaonkar. I was shocked & saddened at her death for she died in the prime of her youth.

2 or 3 months after my arrival in Bombay Khitish rang me up saying that he had a letter for Sabrina to be translated into Italian. I said he was welcome but he never turned up. A year later Suresh Mehta's son told me to come to the new unit at the Gem & Jewellery Complex, Seepz for Stefano, the boss, Stefano,the diamond setter & Piero were coming for a days inspection of the works before the opening ceremony in Deepawali. I went there & met the 3 Italians then I met Khitish & asked him why he didn't come for the translations, his face clouded with sadness. He said he was madly in love with Sabrina. But it was only a one way traffic. All of a sudden his face brightened up saying that he was now engaged to marry a lovely Bengali girl.

PART 3

AS A TEACHER OF
FOREIGN LANGUAGES

CHAPTER 12

TRADE WINGS INSTITUTE OF MANGMT. BOMBAY

In 1999 I turned 63. With the exuberance of youth & the endurance of middle age forever gone, old age had set in & with it began the slow process of the slowing down of physical mobility. I bid adieu to interpreting & translations & turned my attention to my first love which was teaching foreign languages.

Trade wings Institute of Mgmt ran Professional courses in Personality Development, Fashion Designing, Hotel Management,Travel & Tourism & Foreign Languages. They had 4 centres at Thane, Bandra, Andheri & Borivili. The Director was Sunil Rao, Secretary Anita and treasurer Subramanian besides the 4 counsellors one at each centre.

I started teaching French to 4 students at Thane towards the end of April. Presently I started taking classes at the other 3 centres. I bought a Quarterly First class pass to enable me to travel with some degree of comfort.

From the very outset I kept my distance from my students & my classes were very formal. In spite of this I came across my first heckler while I was teaching Spanish at Borivili. He came from one of those rich communities in Kandivili. He started by asking me simple questions,then said that there was no difference between Spanish & English as both had same script, quiet a few words were similar like habitacion in Spanish meant room in English, then he went on to say that what the counsellor promised that he could speak fluently after the course was not a fact & still you people charge a lot of money as fees. At this I lost my temper. I closed my textbook with the bank stepping down the podium marched towards him menacingly. There I stared down at him, his gaze wavered & looked down at his textbook. When he left that evening after class I saw his bag for the last time.

The policy pursued by the management in enrolling students for the language courses was purely mercenary. Their only goal was to make as much money as possible without the least care that the students learnt. 4 clear incidents which I observed when I was there convinced me that the management had no professional interest at all in the student.

I was taking a German class at Bandra & there were 4 students. One of the girls asked me if it was conversational German. I replied that the conversation will come at the end. At first we were doing pronunciation & grammar. She replied that she had done all this at Goethe Institute. The Counsellor clearly told her that it was total conversation & this was the first session. So I allowed her to go to seek clarification from the Counsellor. She never returned. The next incident was at Borivili. This was a Spanish class & we were almost at the end of the course when I saw a new student among the group. He was wearing jeans & the t-shirt. He said he came from California for holidays & he wanted to learn Spanish during his stay in India. The Counsellor told him that today was the first session. I stared at him saying that we are at the end of the course. He got up very furious & I heard him shouting at the Counsellor. The third incident was also in Borivili. I just finished the class & was leaving when a student got up sitting in front of the Counsellor asking me when I was going to start Arabic classes. I stared at the Counsellor in disbelief. "What is going around here" I asked. She replied "all I told him was that there is a faculty for Arabic & language teacher is trying to find a teacher for it & that he should meet you." I told her to stop all that nonsense & to return his fees.

The fourth incident was in Andheri. I was sitting in front of the Counsellor waiting for the class to fill up when the phone rang. She bent her head & started speaking in a whisper. Then suddenly she raised her voice saying 'yes, yes, you would speak fluently at the end of 24 sessions'. I couldn't believe my ears. I told her no one can speak a language fluently after 24 sessions. Its all a big lie. She looked around surreptitiously saying that this was a policy laid down by Mr Sunil Rao. She removed a big book with a blue edge like the one kept by the grain merchants & small businessman. She first wrote the name of the student & the phone number & it was her duty to ring up the student everyday using all devices at her command like pestering, cajoling telling that it is the last chance to join & the next course will be in another 4 months. Carry on this way till the student threatens you for nuisance call.

The salaries of the teachers also were problematic. I was once in a group with some other teachers. One of them was waving a few cheques saying that a lot money but worthless paper. Another complained that he was paid in time but Subramaniam told him not to put in the account until he got the clearance which normally came before the cheque was going to expire. A third said that he was in a dilemma. If he left he would lose all his arrears. But if he continued the arrears would still keep on growing. I was lucky for all my cheques were drawn on Rupee Co-operative Bank, Thane.

One day in the evening while I was entering the Bandra centre Mr Sunil Rao called me. He normally operated from the Bandra centre where he had a glass cage as his office. He told me to close the door behind me. Then he said that he had some good news for me that he had found a forward trading company in Bandra which dealt in commodities & he added like pork meat. Their business was with America at night time. If I could invest one lakh rupees with the trading company I would get excellent returns in the form of 5000 rupees on the Friday after the realisation of my cheque. Thus in 20 weeks my money would be back as interest with the capitol of one lakh still intact. What happened next is very difficult for me to explain. I was mesmerized, hypnotised & blinded by greed. I hardly realised that I was bitten by avarice one of the 7 deadly sins. I gave my cheque and the Friday after the cheque was realised I received a fresh bundle of 100 notes of 50 rupees each. I was ecstatic. For the rest of the week I slept badly dreaming all the time of 50 rupees note dropping in to my lap.

When I went the next Friday to Mr Sunil Rao's glass cage Anita was seated in front of him. A cold chill ran down my spine. I knew that I was conned. I listened to Sunil Rao saying that markets were down & Anita confirming

& corroborating all that he said in a silken soft voice. I heard it all as if from a distant fog. The moment I was out I swung into action. I went to Jerome Saldanha my family lawyer who had his office in Bandra. He listened to my story with a patriarchal smile & said "D'Souza,how could you be so naive as to be taken in by this simple ruse. If what Sunil Rao told you were true Tata's & Ambani's would be queuing outside his office not with one lakh but with several lakhs of rupees. He said use diplomacy to get the money back. I took the receipt for 300 hundred rupees which was his fees & kept it in my briefcase & went straight to my bank manager of Centurion Bank. He was kind enough to give me photo copies of my cheque & other transfer documents. I found my cheque was credited in Bandra branch of the Global Trust Bank to the favour of Cosmos Trading Company - Ravi Soans. I went home & rummaged to my paper clippings & found a Sunday Times Report of entitle EOW (Economic Offense Wing) investigates fraud I read it & found to be the apt clipping. I sat at my type writer for nearly 2 hours drafting a letter addressed to Ravi Soans saying that under instructions from my lawyer Jerome Saldanha I would denounce Ravi Soans to the EOW branch of Bandra police & have him arrested.

Ravi Soans was in Mangalore with his wife expecting the delivery of their first child. He rushed back to Bombay & asked me to meet him. He told me that the one lakh rupees had been made into equity shares in favour of Sunil Rao & nothing could be done. But he would see that within a weeks time I would get 50000 rupees delivered to my house by one of his officers. The balance 45 would be paid at the rate of 5000 a week to be completed in 9 weeks. At the end of it I was left with personal 4 cheques for 30000 rupees which had to be return off. When I turned to teaching I was looking for adventure instead it turned out to be misadventure because of a maverick adventurer. In retrospect Sunil Rao once told me in front of Anita that he had just come from Fort area where he had seen a big room for his fourth centre. On another occasion he told me that he was going to get Aishwarya Ray to join my French classes. He was trying to play the VIP card & the Mangalore connection. Thus he was trying to make up for himself the case for his financial credibility & professional integrity.

P.S. The above eleven chapters cover a period of 32 years from 1967 to 1999. These constitute only a fraction of jobs done by me. They were chosen on the basis of the importance of the Company, that they represent different Industries & are located in different places. Of the remainder I wish to mention 8 jobs which I consider to be of some significance. They are given with the names of the concerned officers within brackets.

1. Several visits to Digjam Woollen Mills, Jamnagar (Goswamy & Aggarwal). 2. Visit to OCM, Amritsar (Ratke). 3. H R Johnson Tiles, Dewas (Kotian & Joshi). 4. For AFCONS,Bombay (Shetty) in their piling contract for Kudremukh Iron Ore Project. 5. For Indage, Bombay (Chowgule & Subramanium) manufacture of sparkling wines (in French). 6.Garware Plastics & Polyesters,Nashik (Murthy & Anantnarayanan). 7. For T.C.I, Bombay (Patel) drawing up of a road map for a forth coming Italian Safari through India. 2 Italians, Mr Fitter (a T.C.I driver) & I started from Oberoi hotel in an Alpha Romeo Car fitted with the map drawing equipment. We went to

Aurangabad (Ajanta & Ellora Caves), Gunar, Indore, Delhi, Agra (Taj Mahal), Rajasthan (Jaipur,Udaipur,Bikaner,Ja isalmer) & along the Gujarat Coast & Western Express Highway,Maharashtra & back to Oberoi. 8. T.C.I.,Bombay (Patel) & Maharashtra Tourism Development Corp. A South India tour for 90 Italians. We went to Madras (Mahabalipuram & Kanchipuram, Bangalore, Mysore, Belur, Halebid (Gomateshwara).

CHAPTER 13

EURO SCHOOL OF FOREIGN LANGUAGES, THANE

It was the student of mine who gave me the idea of starting the language School of my own. Thus in 2002, I contacted Just Dial Services & by evening one of the roving Salesman came knocking at my door. He explained to me the working of Just Dial Services & of the advantages of advertising with them. They would make the services offered by my School available to the public on phone & at their Site on Google. Further if I took out a 2 years subscription I would be entitled to a special discount.

The name of my school was Euro School Of Foreign Languages. The languages taught were German, French, Spanish, Italian & Portuguese. The timings were 9 to 1 & 4 to 8. It was a course lasting 24 hours,each session of one hour duration. Ideally it would be a session on alternate days. Since my classes were to be on a one to one basis in case of necessity I could take daily one hour session or one & half hour session on alternate days. Success would be assured only if the student was willing to do 96 hours of revision that is 4 times the hours I take to teach. Still it would be just a trickle. The crystal flow would come later on after 6 or 9 months usage of the language in the country where it is meant to be used. As an added incentive the course material was free of charge. It consisted of 26 sheets of photo copies on superfine bond paper.

Whenever somebody made an enquiry I boasted that my Institute was the only one which has got the credit rating of : CCC with the code number 19131. With the curiosity of the student sufficiently roused they would ask me what this CCC & the code number was. I said the CCC meant my course is Complete, Comprehensive & Conversational, 1 signified one hour of pronunciation,9 signified 9 hours of grammar & 13 signified 13 sessions of conversation on traditional topics like telling the time, going shopping,eating out & 1 signified useful vocabulary like numbers, food & cosmetic items.

One of my first inquirers plied me with questions for almost the quarter of an hour, asking all kinds of clarifications & ending by asking for a demo. I was annoyed about this & told him that I am a professional teacher & not a salesman dealing in Vacuum Cleaners.

One of the gratification of a teacher is when an old students remembers you. One day Mr Hazare rang me up saying that he was charged by his son now studying Hotel Management in Switzerland. Though his lectures were in English, the German I taught him served him very well in a country that is very racist. Whenever he went for walks, shopping or eating out speaking in German with the Swiss made them forget their racial hatred.

Payal Pandey was studying at Franklin Institute as Air Hostess. She first did German with me & 3 or 4 months later came to do Spanish. She is the only student who did 2 courses in my Institute. When she left she gave me a beautiful card & a set of Cross pens.

One of my students was learning Spanish so that she could follow Spanish films being screened by NDTV in the original Spanish. She started asking me innocently & when I explained she would say 'I will have to check it on my internet'. One day she told me that according to a friend of hers who was working in Madrid for 3 years Castellano & Catalan both are the same languages. I exploded with anger at her saying that Castellano is the language that is spoken by every Spaniard & taught in every Spanish Institute. Catalan was the second language of the people of Catalonia. Hence Barcelona the capital of Catalonia people are bilingual. Something like the people of Mangalore & Udipi speak both Kannada & Tullu. I told her that she was the worst student I have ever met & she gathered all her things to leave. I stopped her & said to finish her class & go. When she left my wife said that she had lost interest in Spanish & she took interest in her cooking. Every time she entered the house she would ask "what are you cooking Aunty & asked her for the recipe ?".

The final tally was for the 7 years teaching 2002 to 2009. French was very much in demand because its a beautiful language. Then came Spanish for diverse reasons : one girl was very impressed by Ricky Martins Song UNO, DOS, TRES. Another girl was fond of Salsa Dance. A Gentleman was exporting memorabilia to Madrid. Third language in demand was Portuguese : Aloknath opened a Ranbaxy office in Saopaolo (Brazil), Dr Padma & Medha Divanji from J K Group learned Portuguese because the group was exporting animal feed to Saopaolo, one man had business interest in Maputo (Mozambique), another Gentleman went to Angola to expand his companies business in that African Country. German was mostly learnt by students going to Switzerland for Hotel Management & IATA Courses. Finally Italian was mostly learnt by married woman waiting to join their husbands working in Milan, Turin & Padua.

Teaching Foreign languages is not as lucrative as doing interpreting or translations. But it has its own rewards. Its a good antidote against loss of memory with aging because of plethora of words the teacher is called upon to remember. It is a good stimulant to the brain because the teacher is called upon to exercise his or her thinking process to the extreme in order to explain the intricacies of grammar. Above all it is the elixir of life so desperately sought after by the Alchemists of the middle ages in their quests for youth & longevity. Teaching youth one gets infected with youthfulness. Since my classes were on one to one basis I often used it as a forum for discussion of ideas. Since most of my students were female I enjoyed engaging them in light & frolicsome banter. At the end of 7 years I was still young at heart & fully refreshed & rejuvenated.

EPILOGUE

VISION, AUSTRALIA

In 2009 at the age of 73, I retired. I had now nothing more to do with languages. I withdrew from the gruelling & often bruising rat race. But at heart I still remained a Vagabond. I spent the next 5 years (2009 – 2014) at my daughters family house in Berwick. Until I returned definitely to India to stay in my home town of Thane.

Berwick is a quiet place, far from the madding crowd & free of all pollution. Its weather is bracing & invigorating. Berwick reminded one of Khandala in 60's & 70's when Khandala was a famous health resort & was well known for its many Sanatoria.

I lived in Berwick like a hermit in silence & solitude passing my days in contemplation, introspection & retrospection. One day while I was switching channels on my walkman radio I came across the channel Vision Australia. I was excited about the services it offered to the people with low vision & the blind. I was specially enthralled by its free talking books library. I filled in the requisite assessment form & submitted it to Vision Australia. Within a week

I received a DAISY player with 2 talking books one was George Elliot's Adam Bede & Richard Woodman 1848.

That revived in me my long abiding passion for reading books. It started in 1946 at the age of 10 when I borrowed my first St. Xaviers High School library book entitled On the road to Mandalay. The book was so absorbing & gripping that I stood on my first floor chawl tenement window, & when my folks were asleep, by the gas light that streamed into the book I read the book till early morning. It was the story of temple priests pursuing some thieves that stole some jewels. Then they pursued the thieves across Mandalay in Burma & the Irawady. Many years later I read a similar novel by Wilkie Collins called The Moonstone.

The next best book I read was the French novel Pecheur D'Islande by Pierre Lotti. It is the tender love story of a fisherman for his village bell which ended tragically when the fisherman goes on a fishing expedition to Iceland but never returns. It was one of the books recommended for my reading for my French Diploma in 1964.

The third best book I have read was Feodor Dostvisky 's Crime & Punishment. Whenever I went outstation on an interpreting job Crime & Punishment was one of the essential items that went with my shaving kit & my tooth brush in my bag. And the fourth book is of recent times the third of the trilogy by the Swedish writer Stieg Larson called The Girl Who Kicked Up The Hornet's Nest. It is a brilliantly translated into immaculate English & is a story of treachery, conspiracy in high places.

Whenever I used to go for a walk on Thane Station road I stopped at the vendor of second hand books. He used to spread his books on a wooden box & here I bought books for Rupees 3 to 5. Thus I made an excellent collection of the following books Charles Dikens A Tale Of 2 Cities, W. Somerset Maugham's of Human Bondage, Thomas Hardy's The Mayor Of Castor Bridge, Sir Author Conan Doyle's The Hound Of Baskerville, Grahan Green's The Power & The Glory, Fredrick Forsyth's The Day Of The Jackal.

Later on I joined the circulatory library on Gokhale road & here I read almost the complete stories of James Hadley Chase with such magical titles as No Orchids For Miss Blendish, U Find Him I Will Fix Him, A.J. Cronim's The Citadel & Hatter's Castle, the Veteranian James Herriot's Delightful Tales Of Animal Life.

With Vision Australia it was a veritable bonanza of books. Almost the entire literary novels of Charles Dikens, a large number of Wilbur Smith's Adventure novels based in South Africa, Earnest Heningway's A farewell To Arms & For Whom The Bell Tolls, John Steinbeck's Grapes Of Wrath & East Of Eden, Evelyn Waugh's Brides Head Revisited & His Complete Collection Of Diaries & Letters, Edgar Allan Poe's Tales Of Mystery & Imagination & Sir Author Conan Doyle's (Sherlock Holmes) 4 novels & 56 cases.

I wish to end these memoirs with a big thank you to Vision Australia. But for their talking books I would be still groping & floundering in a world of total darkness. When both my outward eyes were down they opened for me the inward eye of which speaks the poet William Wordsworth.

For oft when on my couch I lie
In vacant or in pensive mood
They flash upon the inward eye
Which is the bliss of Solitude
And then my heart with pleasure fills
And dances with the Daffodils.